LEADER'S GUIDE

Dr. Katheryn Pfisterer Darr, the writer of this leader's guide, is Associate Professor of Hebrew Bible at Boston University School of Theology. Dr. Darr has written two books, *Far More Precious than Jewels: Perspectives on Biblical Women* and *Isaiah's Vision and the Family of God* (Westminster/John Knox, 1991, 1994). She is on the editorial board for *The New Interpreter's Bible* (Abingdon, 1994 and later) and is writing the commentary on the Book of Ezekiel for this series.

Dr. Darr is a popular speaker at United Methodist pastor and lay conferences throughout the country. She and her husband, Dr. John A. Darr, have a son, Joshua.

ISAIAH, JEREMIAH, LAMENTATIONS

Copyright © 1995 by Cokesbury

All rights reserved.

JOURNEY THROUGH THE BIBLE: ISAIAH, JEREMIAH, LAMENTATIONS. LEADER'S GUIDE. An official resource for The United Methodist Church prepared by the General Board of Discipleship through the Division of Church School Publications and published by Cokesbury, The United Methodist Publishing House; 201 Eighth Avenue, South; P. O. Box 801; Nashville, Tennessee 37202-0801. Printed in the United States of America.

Scripture quotations in this publication, unless otherwise indicated, are from the New Revised Standard Version of the Bible, copyrighted © 1989 by the Division of Christian Education of the National Council of the Churches of Christ in the United States of America, and are used by permission. All rights reserved.

For permission to reproduce any material in this publication, call 615-749-6421, or write to Permissions Office; 201 Eighth Avenue, South; P. O. Box 801, Nashville, Tennessee 37202-0801.

To order copies of this publication, call toll free: 800-672-1789. Call Monday through Friday, 7:00–6:30 Central Time; 5:00–4:30 Pacific Time; Saturday, 9:00–5:00. You may FAX your order to 800-445-8189. Telecommunication Device for the Deaf/Telex Telephone: 800-227-4091. Automated order system is available after office hours. Use your Cokesbury account, American Express, Visa, Discover, or MasterCard.

EDITORIAL TEAM

Mary Leslie Dawson-Ramsey,
Editor

Norma L. Bates,
Assistant Editor

Linda O. Spicer,
Adult Section Assistant

DESIGN TEAM

Ed Wynne,
Layout Designer

Susan J. Scruggs,
Design Supervisor,
Cover Design

ADMINISTRATIVE STAFF

Neil M. Alexander,
Vice-President, Publishing

Duane A. Ewers,
Editor of Church School Publications

Gary L. Ball-Kilbourne,
Senior Editor, Adult Publications

Art and Photo Credits: pp. 9, 50, Charles Shaw; p.22, by courtesy of the Trustees of the British Museum; Copyright British Museum.

 Cokesbury

09 10 11 12 13 – 18 17 16 15 14 13 12 11 10 9 8 7 6 5 4

THIS PUBLICATION IS PRINTED ON RECYCLED PAPER

CONTENTS

Volume 7: Isaiah, Jeremiah, Lamentations
by Dr. Katheryn Pfisterer Darr

$\mathcal{I}$NTRODUCTION TO THE SERIES

The leader's guides provided for use with JOURNEY THROUGH THE BIBLE make the following assumptions:
- adults learn in different ways:
  - —by reading
  - —by listening to speakers
  - —by working on projects
  - —by drama and roleplay
  - —by using their imaginations
  - —by expressing themselves creatively
  - —by teaching others
- the mix of persons in your group is different from that found in any other group;
- the length of the actual time you have for teaching in a session may vary from thirty minutes to ninety minutes;
- the physical place where your class meets is not exactly like the place where any other group or class meets;
- your teaching skills, experiences, and preferences are unlike anyone else's.

We encourage you to discover and develop the ways you can best use the information and learning ideas in this leader's guide with your particular class. To get started, we suggest you try following these steps:

1. Think and pray about your individual class members. Who are they? What are they like? Why are they involved in this particular Bible study class at this particular time in their lives? What seem to be their needs? How do you think they learn best?

2. Think and pray about your class members as a group. A group takes on a character that can be different from the particular characters of the individuals who make up that group. How do your class members interact? What do they enjoy doing together? What would help them become stronger as a group?

3. Keep in mind that you are teaching this class for the sake of the class members, in order to help them increase in their faithfulness as disciples of Jesus Christ. Teachers sometimes fall prey to the danger of teaching in ways that are easiest for themselves. The best teachers accept the discomfort of taking risks and stretching their teaching skills in order to focus on what will really help the class members learn and grow in their faith.

4. Read the chapter in the study book. Read the assigned Bible passages. Read the background Bible passages, if any. Work through the Dimension 1 questions in the study book. Make a list of any items you do not understand and need to research further using such tools as Bible dictionaries, concordances, Bible atlases, and commentaries. In other words, do your homework. Be prepared with your own knowledge about the Bible passages being studied by your class.

5. Read the chapter's material in the leader's guide. You might want to begin with the "Additional Bible Helps," found at the *end* of each chapter in the leader's guide. Then look at each learning idea in the "Learning Menu."

6. Spend some time with the "Learning Menu." Notice that the "Learning Menu" is organized around Dimensions 1, 2, and 3 in the study book. Recognizing that different adults and adult classes will learn best using different teaching/learning methods, in each of the three dimensions you will find
   - —at least one learning idea that is primarily discussion-based;
   - —at least one learning idea that begins with a method other than discussion, but which may lead into discussion.

   Make notes about which learning ideas will work best given the unique makeup and setting of your class.

7. Decide on a lesson plan: Which learning ideas will you lead the class members through when? What materials will you need? What other preparations do you need to make? How long do you plan to spend on a particular learning idea?

8. Many experienced teachers have found that they do better if they plan more than they actually use during a class session. They also know that their class members may become frustrated if they try to do too much during a class session. In other words
   - —plan more than you can actually use. That way, you have back-up learning ideas in case something does not work well or something takes much less time than you thought.
   - —don't try to do everything listed in the "Learning Menu." We have intentionally offered you much more than you can use in one class session.
   - — be flexible while you teach. A good lesson plan is only a guide for your use as you teach people. Keep the focus on your class members, not your lesson plan.

9. After you teach, evaluate the class session. What worked well? What did not? What did you learn from your experience of teaching that will help you plan for the next class session?

May God's Spirit be upon you as you lead your class on their *Journey Through the Bible*!

THE VISION OF ISAIAH

Isaiah 1:1–2:4

Dimension 1: What Does the Bible Say?

(A) Hold an opening worship time.

● Begin your class time with a few moments of silence. Close this centering time with a prayer.

Suggested prayer:
O God of the prophets,
let Your Spirit's presence be with us today.
Open our ears to hear again the words of Isaiah.
In us let the prophet's words live again.
Amen.

(B) Learn about the formation of the Book of Isaiah.

● Prior to class time read the "Additional Bible Helps" found on page 6 of this leader's guide.
● For this learning option you will need to gather various Bible translations (many Bibles have brief introductions prior to each book), Bible dictionaries, and one-volume Bible commentaries. (If you are not familiar with some of these resources, read "Additional Bible Helps," page 16 for a brief overview.) You will also need paper and pencils or pens for each class member.
● Divide class members into groups of three or four. Provide paper and pens or pencils for the groups.
● Ask the groups to read "The Political Situation" and "Isaiah: A Work in Progress" on pages 7–8 of the study book. After they have had a chance to read this information ask them to
—identify major sections in the Book of Isaiah and write this on a piece of paper;
—list information about authorship;
—discuss the time frame in which the book is thought to have been written;
—discuss the purposes addressed by the prophetic writings;
—discuss to whom the book was initially addressed.
● Encourage class members to keep their notes from this

exercise, for they will be a valuable resource throughout this unit on Isaiah.

- After ten minutes, ask a representative from each group to share its findings with the class as a whole.

(C) Answer Dimension 1 questions.

- Remind people that they can enhance their Bible study by reading and completing these questions prior to class. If they have already done so, you can spend a brief amount of time together sharing and discussing answers.
- If class members have not worked through the questions prior to class, you may wish to allow them a few minutes to read the Bible text for the day, along with the questions, either individually or in teams.
- The discussion of Dimension 1 questions might raise the following issues:

1. Isaiah's vision begins with parent/child imagery, then quickly shifts to livestock imagery. Family imagery invites us to perceive the relationship between God and Israel as an intimate, strong, and lifelong bond. In this context, we think of parental love and frustration, as well as youthful rebelliousness and disobedience. (In subsequent chapters, family imagery will continue to be an important feature of Isaiah's vision.)

   Animal imagery also stresses Israel's lack of obedience (even livestock knows its owner), but Israel gives no thought to its God. We can be sure that the author's audience found the application of such imagery to Israel distasteful—even insulting.

   In Isaiah 1:10, the poem addresses Israel's leaders and the nation as "rulers of Sodom" and "people of Gomorrah." Obviously, the poet is willing to use harsh language in order to drive his point home!

2. Isaiah 1 roundly criticizes sinful Judah, especially its leaders, for acts of injustice, oppression, and deceit. God expresses amazement that Israel persists in its rebelliousness, despite the consequences it has suffered.

   Yet condemnation is by no means the only word. Chapter 1 also extends an invitation to faithless Israel to turn its life around. There is no "cheap grace" here, but forgiveness and reconciliation are possible if repentance is genuine.

3. Those in Zion who repent of Israel's long-lived rebelliousness and live in obedience to God, the text promises, will be redeemed by justice and righteousness.

4. Isaiah 2:2-4 (note the superscription in 2:1, reminiscent of 1:1) envisions Zion's exaltation among the nations, whose peoples stream to the city to receive Yahweh's (the LORD's) instruction and who anticipate a future age of peace.

(D) Experience the beginning of Isaiah's vision.

- Ask people to sit quietly, their feet on the floor, arms relaxed, and eyes closed.
- Ask them to listen as you read verses from Isaiah 1 and to visualize the images and actions conveyed in these passages. In a calm voice slowly read the following Scripture texts aloud: 1:1-9, 18-20, 27-31.
- When you have finished reading, give class members several minutes to reflect silently on what they have seen through their mind's eye.
- Then, encourage persons to discuss their experiences of Isaiah's vision with a partner.
- After five minutes, provide an opportunity for several people to share their perceptions with the entire class.

(E) Take a closer look at *vision*.

- For this learning option you will need to have available for your class members: Bibles, concordances, commentaries, and Bible dictionaries.
- Divide class members into groups of three or four members each.
- Ask them to learn as much as they can about the meaning of *vision* in the Hebrew Bible (Old Testament). Encourage groups to use the concordances, commentaries, and other resources you have gathered for this activity.
- At the end of ten minutes, ask a spokesperson from each group to share what the group has learned with the rest of the class.

(F) Examine what it means for Isaiah to be a product of many hands.

Many people simply assume that the entire Book of Isaiah was authored by the eighth-century prophet. Contemporary biblical scholars, however, have amassed an enormous body of evidence to support the view that the Book of Isaiah was a "work in progress" for centuries.

- Divide class members into groups of three or four, and ask them to discuss the following questions:
  —What do we gain when we recognize that the Book of Isaiah was studied, supplemented, and shaped for hundreds of years by faithful communities struggling to discern the meaning of Isaian oracles in light of their own circumstances?
  —What does this ongoing process mean for contemporary teaching of the Book of Isaiah? Are we, too,

called to reinterpret Isaiah in light of our own cultural/social presuppositions, knowledge, and circumstances, even though actual additions to the text are no longer possible?

—In your reading and studying of the Book of Isaiah, have these "living words" spoken out to you? If so which passages, and what concerns have they addressed?

● Groups should be given the opportunity to share with other class members one or two points arising from their discussion.

(G) Illustrate Isaiah's vision.

● For this learning option you will need to have magazines (including news magazines), posterboard or large sheets of paper, scissors, glue, and markers.

● Divide participants into groups of three, and provide each group with the art supplies.

● Encourage each group to make a collage that captures the multifaceted beginning of Isaiah's vision (Isaiah 1:1–2:4).

● Groups can display their artwork in the classroom for the remainder of the unit on Isaiah.

(H) Explore the prophets' use of military imagery.

Surrounded by powerful empires, the small kingdoms of Judah and Israel sought stability and security from many sources—divine assistance, international treaties, political intrigues.

The Book of Isaiah constantly urges Israel to repent of misplaced allegiance and to trust only its God for national security and protection in times of trouble. The biblical authors frequently use military imagery to reassure their audiences of Yahweh's power, protection, and sovereignty over Israel's enemies.

● Read several of the Scripture passages concerning Yahweh's "plan" for Israel and the nations. You will find these passages listed on pages 9–10 of the study book.

● Divide class members into smaller groups of three or four members each to discuss the impact of military imagery on Israel's depictions of God:

—How can we understand the functions of such imagery and ideas, given ancient Israel's precarious national context?

—What do you think about the use of military language in sermons, hymns, and other aspects of Christian worship? What does it contribute? Does its presence raise potential problems? What kind of problems?

(I) Consider the relationship between Israel and God.

Beyond the verses of Chapter 1, Isaiah's vision holds out countless offers of divine forgiveness and reconciliation, if only the people of Israel will turn away from their sins and live according to God's will. Yet already in Chapter 1, those who persist in disobedience are warned of its ultimate consequences. (This tension between divine grace and divine punishment appears in the pages of our New Testament as well.)

At the end of the twentieth century, we may feel uncomfortable speaking of divine judgment. Indeed, the people of ancient Israel may have found such talk uncomfortable as well!

● Divide class members into conversation groups of two or three persons. Ask them, in light of their reading of Isaiah 1:1–2:4, to consider the following questions:

—What do these verses tell us about God?

—What do these verses tell us about human nature?

—What do these verses tell us about our relationship with God?

—What do these verses tell us about our relationships with other men and women?

(J) Paraphrase the beginning of Isaiah's vision.

● Provide class members with paper and pencils or pens.

● Remind persons that putting a biblical text in their own words helps bring its meaning for their lives into sharper focus.

● Ask participants to paraphrase 1:1–2:4 while remaining faithful to the ideas these verses express. If this whole section seems too much, ask the class members to select sections that are meaningful to them.

● After ten minutes, ask one or two class members to share portions of their paraphrases with the entire class.

(K) Anticipate the outcome of Isaiah's vision.

In Isaiah 1, God's prophet lodges charges against Israel, the LORD's rebellious children. Taking into consideration both those charges and the repeated offers of reconciliation, imagine what the ultimate outcome of Isaiah's vision might be.

● Ask class members to share answers to the following

questions with the person sitting next to each of them:

—What do you think is God's hope for Israel's future?

—What do you think Israel's response or responses will be?

—What do you think is God's hope for our future?

—What can you do to further the fulfillment of that hope?

● After eight to ten minutes, encourage participants to share some of their comments with the class as a whole.

(L) Invite your pastor's participation.

● Prior to class time invite your pastor to visit your next class session.

● Explain to your pastor that you are beginning a new study on the Book of Isaiah and one of the learning options will be working with Isaiah 1:10-17. This passage speaks of the importance for acts of worship to be rooted in acts of justice and faithfulness.

● Invite your pastor to speak to your class members about his or her efforts to combine the church's rituals and other acts of worship with the daily lives and practices of congregants beyond sanctuary walls.

● Ask your class members to remember worship services that were specifically oriented to highlighting acts of justice.

—Were these services "special events" (like a mission team going overseas)? Or were these services lectionary based? (The lectionary is a list of Scripture passages assigned to each Sunday of the year. If the lectionary Scripture suggestions are followed for worship, by the end of the three-year cycle the major themes and stories of the Bible will have been used in worship.)

—Why do class members remember these worship services specifically?

—What role can the church play in helping persons integrate their religious beliefs with their everyday lives?

(M) Close with worship.

● If class members enjoy singing you could sing "Behold a Broken World" (*The United Methodist Hymnal*, 426). This may be an unfamiliar hymn to some people. If this is the case you could have different people read the stanzas aloud. The text for the hymn is based on Isaiah 2:1-4.

Additional Bible Helps

Isaiah—Prophetic Voices in Turbulent Times

The Book of Isaiah took shape over tumultuous centuries in Israel's history. During the eighth century B.C., the mighty Assyrian army threatened the existence of both the Northern and Southern Kingdoms. By 721 B.C. the Northern Kingdom had fallen victim to Assyrian aggression, and Judah had become Assyria's vassal state. The eighth-century prophet Isaiah warned his audiences of both outcomes, blaming these tragedies on Israel's faithlessness.

Over a century later, after Assyria's collapse, the Babylonian Empire threatened tiny Judah's existence. In 587 B.C. Jerusalem was sacked and burned, and many of its inhabitants were exiled to Babylon. *How could this have happened?* The people of Judah had believed that a descendant of King David would sit on the throne in Jerusalem forever. They had held fast to the conviction that the Temple, built by Solomon hundreds of years earlier, would never be destroyed. Now, the Davidic king had been carried off in chains to Babylonia, and the Temple was a heap of smoldering ruins. *What hope remained for Israel?*

Decades of despair passed. Near the end of the Babylonian exile, however, an anonymous prophet (the so-called "Second Isaiah") announced the exiles' imminent return to Jerusalem. As we shall see, his oracles proclaimed that Cyrus, king of Persia, was marching toward Babylon at Yahweh's command and that the exiles would be allowed to return to a restored and Eden-like homeland. The Second Isaiah portion of Isaiah's vision (Chapters 40–55) insists that Judah's past sins warranted its punishment, but it also offers wholesale forgiveness to all in exile who do not turn aside to worship deities other than Yahweh.

The exiles who returned to Jerusalem in response to Cyrus's liberating edict discovered no Eden there. The city lay in ruins. Those who had remained in Judah during the years of Babylonian exile were by no means certain that this sudden return of their former countrymen and women meant good news for them. Resources were scarce, and drought and famine were recurring problems. Increasingly, the Jewish community was threatened by conflicts among its members and poor relations with surrounding peoples. The Third Isaiah corpus (large body of writing of a specific kind, Isaiah 56–66) describes these discouraging circumstances, all the while urging those faithful to God to anticipate the final outworking of Yahweh's plan for Israel and the nations.

Throughout the history of its composition, then, editors and later prophets supplemented the existing Isaiah of their day with oracles, insights, wrestlings, and hopes. There is much evidence that these individuals, particularly those working during the final stages of the scroll's compilation, sought to shape these disparate materials into a reasonably coherent literary work—the vision of Isaiah. In particular, they labored to bring earlier themes forward into later chapters and especially to retroject later themes into earlier portions of the collection. The recurring theme of God's plan, discussed on pages 9–10 of the study book, probably grew as a result of such reciprocal editorial activity. Our indebtedness to these later prophets and editors is great.

Indeed, without their ongoing efforts, we cannot be sure that earlier portions of the book would have survived.

At points in this chapter, we have emphasized that Isaiah 1:1–2:4 functions to introduce readers to the entire vision of Isaiah—all sixty-six chapters of the book. As Christopher R. Seitz notes in his essay, "Isaiah 1–66: Making Sense of the Whole," our vantage point as readers is both a privilege and a responsibility:

"We know God's full intention for Zion early on (Isa. 2:1-5). But the final chapter of the Isaiah drama has not been written. More so than for the other prophetic collections, Isaiah remains open to the future, and it is doubtless for this reason that Isaiah is the most frequently cited Old Testament prophet in the New Testament. The church proclaimed that the trajectory of Messiah, so prominent in the Isaiah corpus, had reached its culmination in Jesus of Nazareth (Matt. 1:22//Isa. 7:14). But the full restoration of Zion and the cosmos is never accomplished within Isaiah's own literary framework. So too, it remains a lively hope in the New Testament precisely because of the entrance into history of the one proclaimed Christ. The reign of the righteous Davidic scion [descendant] was to usher in the eschatological age of peace and proper justice (Isaiah 9:2-7; 11:6-9). This vision of Isaiah remains God's final will and purpose for the created order, a will and purpose not so much completed in Jesus Christ as sharpened and held out to the present community of faith, both in challenge and in promise." [1]

To the extent that we enter into Isaiah's vision, choosing to remain obedient to God, steadfast in faith, and alive with hope for the ultimate fulfillment of God's plan for the entire created order, Isaiah's vision becomes our own.

---

[1] Seitz's essay appears on pages 105–126 of *Teaching and Preaching the Book of Isaiah*, Christopher R. Seitz, editor (Fortress Press, 1988); this quotation is on page 123.

GOD'S VOICES

DATES	PROPHETS
850 B.C.	Elijah
760–745 B.C.	Amos
755–725 B.C.	Hosea
742–687 B.C.	(Jerusalem) **Isaiah**
722–701 B.C.	Micah
630–620 B.C.	Zephaniah
626–587 B.C.	**Jeremiah**
625–612 B.C.	Nahum
608–598 B.C.	Habakkuk
593–571 B.C.	Ezekiel
after 587 B.C.	Obadiah
540 B.C.	(Second) **Isaiah**
(approximate date) after 540 B.C.	(Third) **Isaiah**
520 B.C.	Haggai
520–518 B.C.	Zechariah
500–450 B.C.	Malachi

2 CONDEMNATIONS AND CALL

Isaiah 5:1–6:13

Based upon your knowledge of class members, their interests and needs, and the learning approaches that work best, choose at least one learning activity from each of the three following Dimensions. Spend approximately one-third of class time working on a Dimension 1 activity. Remember, however, that approximately two-thirds of your time should be spent on activities selected from Dimensions 2 and 3.

Dimension 1: What Does the Bible Say?

(A) Open with a time of worship.

- Begin your session by reading aloud this familiar verse describing Isaiah's call:
  " 'Whom shall I send, and who will go for us?' And I said, 'Here am I; send me!' " (Isaiah 6:8)
- Then sing together "Here I Am, Lord" (*The United Methodist Hymnal*, 593). If you have a pianist or other musician in your class, check with him or her before class starts and ask for musical accompaniment for this hymn.

(B) Answer Dimension 1 questions.

- Remind class members that they can enhance their Bible study by reading and reflecting on these questions prior to class. If they have already worked through the questions in Dimension 1 before class time, spend up to fifteen minutes sharing and discussing responses. If they have not worked through the questions, allow them a few minutes to read the Bible text for the day, along with the questions, either individually or in teams.
- Discussion of Dimension 1 questions might raise the following issues:
1. Isaiah's use of a familiar vintage festival song illustrates that the prophets drew from a variety of sources—love songs, community laments, the language of legal proceedings, and so on—in order to make their oracles more interesting, powerful, or provocative. Unaware of the figures standing behind the vinesman and his vineyard, Isaiah's audience renders a judgment—likely in favor of the vinesman whose patient and persistent labor have not been rewarded. Reaching verse 7, however, the audience discovers that it has rendered judgment *for* God and *against* itself.
2. Isaiah 5:8-10 asserts that those wealthy persons who exploit the poor, depriving them of their land and possessions, will not be able to enjoy the fruits of their dishonest gain. To the contrary, the land and houses they

have seized will be left desolate when they are forcibly removed from the land.

Isaiah 5:14-17 threatens that those leaders (Jerusalem's nobility) who exalt themselves on account of their rank and wealth will be "brought" low, devoured by Sheol (the shadowy, underground dwelling place of the dead). Only the Lord of hosts is exalted in justice and righteousness.

For all these offenses (note "therefore" in 5:25), Yahweh's anger will be manifest among the people and they will suffer military atrocities at the hands of a powerful and fearsome army.

3. The prophet adopts plant imagery in 5:24 in order to convey a vivid sense of the destruction awaiting those who excel at self-serving conspiracies, feeding their egos, consuming excessive amounts of alcohol, and maneuvering their friends out of legal straits, but who refuse to insure the rights of the poor and helpless in their midst.

4. In Isaiah's call experience, he "witnesses" Yahweh enthroned in the midst of the divine council. Isaiah fears for his life and for the lives of his people, since impurity cannot exist in the presence of the Holy God. But a seraph touches his lips with a burning coal, proclaiming that by this process, Isaiah's guilt and sin have been "blotted out."

(C) Compose an accusation and a rebuttal.

- Provide each class member with paper and a pencil or pen.
- Ask each person to write a paraphrase of Isaiah's accusations in Chapter 5 against his audiences—the nation as a whole and its leaders.
- Invite class members to think creatively about what the responses of Isaiah's audiences to his accusations may have been and to write their rebuttal to Isaiah's charges. Remember, people tend to justify their actions rather than admitting that charges lodged against them are true.
- When class members have completed these two tasks, invite them to share their findings with a person sitting next to them or with the class as a whole.

(D) Picture Isaiah's call.

- For this activity you will need paper, colored pencils or markers, scissors, and glue for everyone to use.
- Ask class members to sit comfortably with their eyes closed as you read the account of Isaiah's call experience (6:1-13).
- When you have finished reading, invite them to create a picture of what they saw with their mind's eye as they listened to the reading.
- Those wishing to do so may share their artwork with the

class as a whole. After everyone who wishes to share their picture has done so, you can show the class one artist's rendition of this scene (above).
- Invite willing class members to display their artwork in the classroom for the remainder of the unit of study on Isaiah.

Dimension 2: What Does the Bible Mean?

(E) Read between the lines.

- You will need to have a large sheet of paper and markers or the use of a chalkboard and chalk for this learning option.
- Recruit one member of the class to record responses to the class discussion.
- Read aloud Isaiah 5:8-13, 18-23. In these passages Isaiah lodges serious accusations against his contemporaries. Ask class members to discuss the following questions together:
  —What are the charges against his contemporaries?
  —Based on those charges, what may we conclude that God wished to be the attitudes and actions of those addressed?
  —Are God's wishes recorded here relevant today? Why, or why not?

(F) Investigate Isaiah's vocabulary.

- For this activity you will need Bible dictionaries, concordances, commentaries, paper, and pencils or pens. (See "Additional Bible Helps," page 16 for information on the use of Bible reference books.)
- Share information found in the "Additional Bible Helps"

found at the end of this chapter about "Prophets and Poetry."

- Ask class members, working in pairs, to look up the meanings of unfamiliar words and phrases in Isaiah 5–6.
  —Examples might include *bath, homer, ephah, Sheol, seraphs,* and *terebinth.*
- At the end of ten minutes, survey the pairs for words whose meanings they have learned.
- Ask class members to share where were the surprises in the meanings they found.
  —How does having these Hebrew meanings enrich your understanding of the text?

(G) Discuss the purpose of Isaiah's prophecies.

- Divide class members into three or four small groups.
- Ask them to discuss the following questions:
  —If, as Isaiah was warned, his prophecies met with little or no success, what may have been their function?
  —Why might the preservers of Isaiah's oracles think it important to keep a record of God's announced purposes?
  —Were Isaiah's prophecies in Chapter 5 of a sort that were relevant only to one period in Judah's history? Or may they have retained their relevance beyond the prophet's lifetime?

(H) Imagine Isaiah's predicament.

Isaiah was commissioned to serve as God's mouthpiece to the people of Judah and its capital, Jerusalem. Yet from the time of his commissioning, he knew that his oracles would have no effect.

- Divide the class members into small groups. Ask each group to read Isaiah's call, Isaiah 6:1-13.
- Ask class members to imagine what Isaiah's feelings may have been by having them consider answers to these questions:
  —Did he experience a sense of futility, suspecting that all the work that went into the preparation and delivery of his oracles was meaningless?
  —Did he fear the social alienation and ridicule he was certain to face?
  —Did he sometimes question whether his vision of Yahweh, enthroned among members of the divine council, was real or only a figment of his imagination?
- When people have reflected on these questions in their small groups, ask the groups to roleplay what Isaiah may have been feeling when confronted with the reality of his call from the Lord. Ask the groups to share these ideas with the whole class.

(I) Ask questions of the text.

- Divide class members into conversation groups of two or three persons. Ask them, in light of their reading of Isaiah 5, to consider the following questions:
  —What does this chapter tell us about God?
  —What does it tell us about human nature?
  —What does it tell us about our relationship with God?
  —What does it tell us about our relationships with, and responsibilities to, persons in our communities?
- At the end of ten minutes, ask one person from each group to give the whole class a summary of that group's responses to one of the four questions posed. Be sure that each of the four questions is addressed by one of the groups.

(J) Compare Judah's social ills with ours.

Isaiah identified a number of problems in the Judean society of his day: social injustice, alcoholism, self-absorption, greed, and deceit.

These conditions strongly suggest that the dialogue between God and the people of Judah had broken down because the people had stopped listening to God's revealed will for their lives. They placed themselves first, happy to enjoy the benefits they believed were theirs as the people of Yahweh but refused to honor their responsibilities to God.

Alien though Isaiah's prophecies sometimes seem, his critique of his nation certainly seems appropriate to aspects of our own.

- Ask one member of your group to play the role of Isaiah, God's mouthpiece.
- Ask several other persons to play the role of contemporary leaders in our own society. (You need not attach specific names to these persons.)
- Give the volunteers a few minutes to get their ideas together.
- Provide five minutes for dialogue between "Isaiah" and representatives of our own, twentieth-century situation. What does Isaiah say to our representatives? How do they respond?
- At the end of five minutes, ask if other class members would like to share a different view or other ideas. Allow the dialogue to continue for another few minutes.
- Be sensitive that differing political views may surface during this learning option especially pertaining to social concerns. Try to hear Isaiah's words guiding your discussion.

(K) Discuss how to understand the Old Testament.

- Divide the class into three conversation groups. Ask each group to respond to the statements and questions assigned to it. Feel free to photocopy the following learning option material in order to share the information with the three groups.

Group One

Israel's precarious *geographical location* played a profound role in its history. There were skirmishes and outright wars with the other small kingdoms in its region; and mighty empires, hungry for world conquest and control of valuable trade routes, threatened and ultimately defeated both the Northern and Southern Kingdoms.

—In our day, people living in precarious geographical locales continue the struggle for survival. What factors motivate them to remain in such dangerous circumstances? How can we, as Christians, understand and respond to their plight?

Group Two

Israel's *theocentric* worldview led it to interpret events as the actions of its deity—God rewarded good with good and punished evil with evil. Imagine how different ancient Israel's understanding of its God and of itself might have been had its geographical locale been such that centuries of peace and prosperity passed without interruption.

—When jetliners fall from the sky or an earthquake devastates a city, we do not interpret such acts as God's direct intervention to punish a sinful plane crew or a city's inhabitants. Yet we may, on occasion, tend to "blame God" when things go wrong, or to assume that persons living in desperate circumstances—poverty, addiction, and so on—are somehow less deserving than we of life's blessings. How can we reconcile blaming God for some events and not others? How can we reconcile blaming God for bad things that happen with not giving God praise for the good things that come our way?

Group Three

Ethnocentrism is a prominent feature of much of the literature contained in our Old Testament. Ancient Israel eventually came to regard its God as the supreme deity, the creator of the cosmos whose sovereignty extended to all the world (as they knew it!) and its inhabitants. Yet when Israel viewed the world, it affirmed that this all-powerful God was particularly involved in its own

past, present, and future. While not denying that Yahweh was at work in the events of other nations, Israel placed itself at the very center of God's concern.

—We may wish to affirm that God cares deeply about all the world with its peoples and nations (and perhaps other worlds as well). Yet it is all too easy for us to adopt an ethnocentristic perspective—that is, to assume that God cares more about us, our community of believers, our nation, than about anyone else. How do we exhibit ethnocentrism in our church? in our community? in our nation?

- After ten minutes, invite a spokesperson from each group to summarize its discussion of the topic the group has addressed.

(L) Hold a time of closing worship.

- Share with your class members some of the information found in the "Additional Bible Helps" section, "Isaiah Sides With the Poor" (below).
- "The Voice of God is Calling" (*The United Methodist Hymnal*, 436) would be an excellent closing hymn. You may want to sing the hymn with class members. Another option would be to have different class members read the various stanzas.

Additional Bible Helps

Isaiah Sides With the Poor

Isaiah took to task those inhabitants of Judah and Jerusalem who oppressed the poor and denied justice to the powerless. He dared proclaim God's demands for justice and righteousness to persons whose eyes and ears were closed. They were consumed with greed and self-gratification. How did Isaiah find the courage to speak as he did? Perhaps he was emboldened by the knowledge that his own guilt and sin had been blotted out and that his commission came from no less than the holy and exalted God.

In his hymn written in 1913, "The Voice of God is Calling," John Haynes Holmes expresses his conviction that God summons each of us to take up Isaiah's commission. But he also offers, in the spirit of Isaiah, what our response to God's summons should be:

The voice of God is calling
  its summons in our day;
Isaiah heard in Zion,
  and we now hear God say:
"Whom shall I send to succor
  my people in their need?
Whom shall I send to loosen
  the bonds of shame and greed?

"I hear my people crying
   in slum and mine and mill;
no field or mart is silent,
   no city street is still.
I see my people falling
   in darkness and despair.
Whom shall I send to shatter
   the fetters which they bear?"

We heed, O Lord, your summons,
   and answer: Here are we!
Send us upon your errand,
   let us your servants be.
Our strength is dust and ashes,
   our years a passing hour;
but you can use our weakness
   to magnify your power.

From ease and plenty save us;
   from pride of place absolve;
purge us of low desire;
   lift us to high resolve;
take us, and make us holy;
   teach us your will and way.
Speak, and behold! we answer;
   command, and we obey!
The United Methodist Hymnal, 436

Prophets and Poetry

Sometimes we work so hard to understand the meaning of a prophetic text that we forget to pay attention to the words by which that meaning is conveyed. Yet the two can scarcely be separated. This is particularly true of Israel's prophetic literature, for the prophets were poets who labored over every word in order most effectively to convey God's message in ways that would capture their audiences' attention and convince them of the truth of their assertions. When we take care to notice the prophet's use of poetic techniques, however, the Bible discloses its meaning to us more fully. Consider Isaiah's use of the following poetic techniques and persuasive strategies:

—Isaiah's adoption of a vintage festival song is one example of a strategic use of language. Borrowing what may have been a popular ditty, he concealed the identities of the "beloved" (God) and the vineyard (Judah) until after the inhabitants of Jerusalem and Judah had been invited to judge between them (5:3). At that point, the people discovered that they had actually been asked to judge themselves! (5:7).

—In Hebrew, Isaiah 5:7 contains two wordplays:
   "He expected justice [*mispat*],
      but saw bloodshed [*mispah*];
   righteousness [*sedaqah*],
      but heard a cry [*se`aqah*]!"

—A few verses later, Isaiah characterizes the drunken feasts of those who disregard God (5:11-13). The poetry invites us not only to read the text but also to hear the songs of the lyre, harp, tambourine, and flute that accompanied their drinking parties. Describing their fate, Isaiah personifies Sheol—the underground, shadowy realm of the dead—as a monster that opens wide its mouth to consume Jerusalem's nobility (5:14).

—In 5:18, Isaiah depicts iniquity and sin as heavy burdens that sinners nevertheless drag along, as beasts and humans must drag heavy items placed upon carts.

—Isaiah 5:24 describes the burning of grass that is highly combustible because it is so dry. In our mind's eye, we witness the flames devouring blossoms and leaves, as roots rot in the ground. So, the prophet claims, shall the people become, for they have rejected the Lord's teaching and despised God's word.

—Isaiah 5:26-30 describes, as we have seen, the approach of a fierce enemy army. The prophet focuses upon their clothing, their weapons, and the hoofs of their horses, conveying through these details a vivid sense of their terrifying advance against Judah.

3

Isaiah 7:1–8:15; 12

TRUST IN THE LORD!

Dimension 1:
What Does the Bible Say?

(A) Hold an opening worship time.

> If you have someone in your class who plays the guitar, recruit her or him to play and sing or help lead the singing of the song "Sois la Semilla" ("You Are the Seed") *The United Methodist Hymnal*, 583. A piano accompaniment is available for this hymn. Since this hymn is probably unfamiliar, recruit your musicians early.

● In today's time together you may choose to reflect on what it means to be a prophet. You will have an opportunity to look more closely at the role Isaiah played.

You will be challenged to look for contemporary prophets. The question of "How are we each called to be prophetic?" will hopefully arise. Try to set this mood in your opening time of worship.

● A suggested opening hymn is "Sois la Semilla," *The United Methodist Hymnal*, 583. Close with a prayer asking for God's guidance and direction for today's session; that prophetic words will be heard; and that trust in God will be felt.

(B) Learn more about King Ahaz and the Syro-Israelite crisis.

Second Kings 16 gives another account of the Syro-Israelite crisis (described in Isaiah 7:1–8:15).

● For this learning option you will need various Bible translations, paper, pencils or pens.

● Divide class members into groups of three or four members each.

● Allow time for everyone to read 2 Kings 16 and to read Isaiah 7:1–8:15 if they have not already done so.

● Then ask them to list differences between the account in Second Kings and the account in Isaiah 7:1–8:15.

● Their lists will probably include the following differences:
　—Unlike Isaiah 7:1–8:15, 2 Kings 16 tells us that Ahaz became king when he was only twenty years of age and ruled for sixteen years.

—The Second Kings account charges Ahaz with practicing child sacrifice; that is, he offered his son as a burnt offering, undoubtedly in the midst of a crisis (and in the mistaken hope that doing so would evoke a positive divine response).

—Second Kings 16:5 states that Rezin and Pekah waged war against Jerusalem and besieged it. The next verse states that the king of Edom took advantage of Judah's present plight by regaining control of the city of Elath and driving the Judeans from the territory.

—Unlike the Isaiah account, 2 Kings 16:7 quotes from Ahaz's request that the king of Assyria, Tiglath-pileser, come to his aid. It also tells that when Ahaz went to Damascus to pay homage to Tiglath-pileser, he saw an (Assyrian-style) altar there. Ahaz sent an exact description of the altar to the priest Uriah (yoo-RIGH-uh), commanding that it be duplicated and installed in the Temple in Jerusalem.

—The prophet Isaiah does not appear in 2 Kings 16.

—The account in Second Kings refers to the "Book of the Annals of the Kings of Judah," a royal record of events during the reigns of Judah's kings.

● When groups have completed their lists, they may share their findings with the class as a whole.

(C) Answer the Dimension 1 questions.

● Remind class members that they can enhance their study experience by reading the Bible texts and reflecting on the questions in Dimension 1 prior to class time. If they have already worked through the questions, they can spend ten to fifteen minutes sharing and discussing their findings. If they have not already worked through the questions in Dimension 1, allow a few minutes for Bible reading and reflection on the questions, individually or in teams.

● Discussion of Dimension 1 questions might raise the following points:

1. Isaiah urges King Ahaz to heed his words and not to fear, because the Syro-Israelite alliance will fail. In 7:9b, Isaiah gives Ahaz a warning; in Hebrew, this warning contains a wordplay:

"If you do not stand firm in faith [ta'aminu], you shall not stand at all [te'amenu]."

2. When Ahaz declines Yahweh's offer of a confirming sign, Isaiah informs him that the Lord will send a sign nonetheless. A certain young woman (the queen, perhaps, or Isaiah's wife) will conceive and bear a son, naming him *Immanuel*, meaning "God is with us." Before that child knows how to refuse the evil and choose the good (perhaps a reference to food, though the prophet may be referring to the age when moral discernment becomes possible), both the kingdoms of Syria and Israel will lie deserted. But faithless Judah

will face a crisis even greater than its present dilemma.

3. According to Isaiah 8:4, both Damascus (the capital of Syria) and Samaria (the capital of Israel) would be plundered before Maher-shalal-hash-baz could say a baby's first words, "Daddy" and "Mommy."

4. Isaiah 12 anticipates a time when all Israel will trust in God for its salvation, praising the Lord for all that has been done on its behalf. The city of Zion will be filled with shouts and songs of joy.

Dimension 2: What Does the Bible Mean?

(D) Ponder the prophets in our midst.

● Divide class members into groups of three and four members each.

● Ask them to review the information found in the sidebar in the study book, "Central and Peripheral Prophets," on page 25

● Ask the small groups briefly to discuss where they think the prophet Isaiah would fit best.

● Ask group members to identify persons whom they regard as contemporary prophets.

● Then ask persons in their groups to deal with the following questions:

—Are these contemporary people *peripheral* prophets, *central* prophets, or do they exhibit characteristics of both types of intermediaries?

—In what social and religious contexts might peripheral prophets be especially important and useful?

—In what social and religious contexts might central prophets be especially important and useful?

● Ask the groups to report their ideas and insights to the whole class.

(E) Struggle with how to tell a true prophet from a false one.

● In this learning option class members will work with other Bible texts in which the fulfillment or nonfulfillment of a prophetic word serves as the basis for identifying true and false prophecies.

● You will need Bibles, pens or pencils, and paper for this option.

● Review the section, "Distinguishing Between True and False Prophets," page 16 in the study book. Review this information with class members, or ask them to read the section.

● Divide class members into three working groups.

● Ask each group to read and discuss one of the following biblical texts in which the fulfillment or nonfulfillment criteria appears:

—**Group One:** 1 Kings 22:1-28
—**Group Two:** Jeremiah 28:1-9
—**Group Three:** Ezekiel 33:23-33
- Then ask the small groups to discuss these questions:
—Who are the characters in the passage?
—What historical happenings are being reviewed?
—What are the prophet's words?
—What will be the measure of success of the prophet's words? How will the people know that the prophet's words are of God?
- After ten minutes, invite each group to share its text with the class as a whole.

(F) Write a poem.

- For this learning option you will need paper and pencils or pens for each class member.
- Share the following background information with your class:

  In the view of most biblical scholars, Isaiah 8:9-10 is not from the prophet Isaiah. Rather, these scholars believe this passage to be a later addition to the text. In the midst of materials concerning the Syro-Israelite crisis, these verses proclaim to the nations the futility of conspiring against Israel, since "God is with us." Knowing that Ahaz voiced no such trust and assurance in response to Isaiah's words, we cannot attribute these poetic lines either to him or to his advisers. Rather, some later prophet or editor has inserted an expression of just such confidence and trust as the situation called for but did not evoke from Ahaz.
- Ask a member of the class to read Isaiah 8:9-10.
- Then ask each class member to write his or her own short poem celebrating God's sustaining presence in the midst of crisis.
- At the end of ten minutes, encourage those who are willing to share their poem with the class as a whole. Then ask class members to slip this poem into their Bibles for their personal devotion at a later time.

(G) Draw a vision of peace.

- For this learning option you will need drawing paper, crayons, markers, pencils, scraps of construction paper, glue. (Some optional materials you might include are: glitter, fabrics, feathers.)

  Isaiah's words continue to speak and inspire us. In these days of our war-torn world, where refugees roam trying to find a home, we long for a world where guns will be silent and creation will be at peace.

  What would that world be like to you?
- Encourage individuals to select the creative supplies they need, to spread out and find table space upon which to work. Ask them to listen while Isaiah 11:1-9 is read.
- Then say, "Here is one prophet's vision. What is yours?"

- Give class members at least fifteen minutes to reflect on this and to create a vision of peace. At the end of the time ask those who are willing to share their creations and their thoughts. Be sure to point out the painting by Edward Hicks on page 27 of the study book. Hicks painted many versions of "The Peaceable Kingdom." You may be able to find another version on a Christmas card or in an art book.

Dimension 3:
What Does the Bible Mean to Us?

(H) Explore your level of trust in God.

Experienced leaders can find it very difficult to relinquish control of formidable situations. They are accustomed to "calling the shots," conceiving and implementing strategies based on the resources at their disposal. Such qualities can be essential, of course, to effective leadership. Yet great leaders must also be able to recognize when situations call for patience and for assistance beyond their control.

Whatever Ahaz's relationship with the Lord had been prior to the Syro-Israelite crisis, he was unwilling to trust God's instructions during a period of potential national catastrophe.

- Ask class members to divide into groups of three or four persons each. Each group should address the following statements and questions for approximately ten minutes:
—To what extent are we prepared to be patient and trust in God when crises beyond our control confront us?
—What is the difference between patience and trust on the one hand, and apathy or cowardice on the other?
— When have we/you been like Ahaz?
- At the end of ten minutes, invite a representative from each group to report its responses to the class as a whole.

(I) Imagine yourself as God's prophet.

- Divide class members into discussion groups of three to four persons.
- Allow ten minutes for each group to discuss the following questions:
—Could you play the role of a peripheral prophet in family, church, or business situations if you felt God's call? Why, or why not?
— Can you see yourself playing the role of a central prophet in certain situations? What kind of situation?
—What must prophets be willing to undergo? What would you be willing to experience in order to be God's prophet?
- After ten minutes, invite each group to share its discussion with the entire class.

(J) Close with a time of worship.

- Join in prayers of thanksgiving and praise.
- Invite participants to pray silently about a time when they believe they fell short of God's will for them. After several minutes, lead the class in reciting Isaiah 12:1:

  > "I will give thanks to you, O LORD,
  >> for though you were angry with me,
  > your anger turned away,
  >> and you comforted me."

- Ask persons to pray silently about a time when they have trusted in God, despite uncertainty and fear. After several minutes, lead the class in reciting Isaiah 12:2:

  > "Surely God is my salvation;
  >> "I will trust, and will not be afraid,
  > for the LORD GOD is my strength and my might;
  >> he has become my salvation."

- Allow class members several minutes to offer a silent prayer of thanksgiving to God for some blessing or blessings in their lives. When they have finished, close by reading Isaiah 12:3-6.

Additional Bible Helps

Putting Ourselves in Isaiah's Shoes

The Bible does not tell us many things that we would like to know about Isaiah. Apparently, the compilers of ancient Israel's prophetic traditions were not as interested in the prophets' lives as they were in the words God spoke through them.

Biblical scholars surmise that Isaiah lived in Jerusalem, an educated, influential person who had access even to the king. We know nothing of his father, Amoz (AY-muhz, Isaiah 1:1) or of how Isaiah earned his living. Some scholars suggest that Isaiah was a priest; after all, he was inside the Jerusalem Temple when he received his commission to function as God's spokesperson.

Isaiah's prophetic role influenced his personal life. He gave message names to at least two sons. Indeed, the conception of Maher-shalal-hash-baz occurred at Yahweh's command. No doubt Isaiah's entire head and heart were consumed by the awesome responsibility of communicating God's words to his audiences.

We cannot know the thoughts and feelings that swirled inside Isaiah as he envisioned God enthroned among the seraphs. We cannot ask what thoughts and plans filled his mind as he set out with his son to counsel Ahaz about the Syro-Israelite crisis. But we can imaginatively place ourselves in Isaiah's shoes and consider what might have been his state of mind. Isaiah had been warned that his oracles would have no effect on his audiences. Did he hope, nevertheless, that Ahaz would find the courage to trust in God? Did he fear for his life, should the king become angry at him for announcing that God was going to provide a sign, Ahaz's protests notwithstanding?

We should probably resist Hollywood's tendency to "fill out" the biblical characters with stories having no basis in the text. Yet we can be certain that God's prophets were not robots, speaking words that left them unaffected. Being God's prophet seems often to have placed men and women in the midst of controversy, crisis, uncertainty, and doubt. Recall that in Isaiah 8:12-15, God speaks to Isaiah directly, reminding him to keep his focus on God alone.

When we remember that ancient Israel's prophets were human beings, we begin to catch a glimpse of how great were the tasks set before them and of the courage necessary to undertake those tasks.

BASIC TOOLS FOR BIBLE STUDY

Bible Dictionaries

The world the Bible describes is in many respects an alien world. It is strange because it is unknown. As a careful reader you will not want to gloss over that alien character, to assume too quickly that you know what was going on in those ancient days. More like small-scale encyclopedias than traditional dictionaries, Bible dictionaries have a wealth of information about the people, events, ideas, and books of the Bible.

Bible dictionaries vary in size and depth. The new standard for comprehensive coverage is *The Anchor Bible Dictionary* (Doubleday, six volumes, 1992). *The Interpreter's Dictionary of the Bible* (Abingdon, four volumes, 1962; supplementary volume, 1976) is older but still found in some church libraries. Two solid recent examples of affordable, single-volume dictionaries are *The Dictionary of Bible and Religion*, edited by William H. Gentz (Abing-don, 1986), and *Harper's Bible Dictionary*, edited by Paul J. Achtemeier (Harper and Row, 1985).

Concordances

A concordance to the Bible is another basic tool for Bible study. Many people use a concordance only when they want to look up a half-remembered verse that keeps nagging their memory. But a concordance has a systematic place in Bible study too.

Suppose you want to study a theme such as *redemption*. A concordance will tell you where to find *redemption* in the Bible.

Be sure to select a concordance that you can use with your translation of the Bible. Concordances are available for use with the following versions of the Bible: King James Version, New Revised Standard Version, Revised Standard Version, New International Version, and *Good News Bible: The Bible in Today's English Version*.

Bible Handbooks

Bible handbooks help keep you from losing sight of the forest while in the trees. They typically present a thumbnail sketch of the content and context of each book of the Bible. Most versions also include essays on all sorts of background material on various subjects from ancient measures, weights, money, and calendars to ancient manuscripts to archaeology. Two examples with somewhat different theological slants are *Eerdmans' Handbook to the Bible*, edited by David Alexander and Pat Alexander (Eerdmans, 1983) and *The Illustrated Bible Handbook*, by Edward P. Blair (Abingdon, 1987). The latter is out of print but found in some church libraries. A helpful recent volume, which serves some of the same purposes as a handbook, is *A Beginner's Guide to the Books of the Bible*, by Diane L. Jacobson and Robert Kysar (Augsburg/Fortress, 1991).

Books That Introduce the Bible

General introductions weave history into the explanations about the content and development of the Scriptures. These introductions give one a sense of the big picture within which a particular passage is located. Bernhard W. Anderson's much-used *Understanding the Old Testament* is now in its fourth edition (Prentice-Hall, 1986). I also like Peter C. Craigie's *The Old Testament: Its Background, Growth, and Content* (Abingdon, 1986). Craigie takes special pains to explain where and why conservative and liberal biblical scholars disagree. For the New Testament, James L. Price's *The New Testament: Its History and Theology* (Macmillan, 1987) is a standard reference work. Other good options are also in print.

Bible Atlases

Another type of resource that can help is an atlas of Bible lands. Even a quick look at a map can help you place a biblical passage in a geographic location and therefore make better sense of it. You may, for example, be able to picture the setting of Psalm 137 when you see how far Babylon was from Jerusalem.

Many Bible-map resources are available. Probably the standard reference is the *Oxford Bible Atlas*, third edition, edited by Herbert G. May (Oxford University Press, 1985). The twenty-six detailed maps are accompanied by short essays explaining the linkages to biblical texts and general background. More ambitious readers may want to peruse *The Harper Atlas of the Bible*, edited by James B. Pritchard (Harper and Row, 1987), which is available in oversized and concise editions.

Commentaries

What about commentaries on the Bible? There is no question that commentaries can help you. But they can be dangerous, too, in a couple of ways. First, you can easily become dependent on commentaries and never do the homework necessary to know a text for yourself. Second, when you lean heavily on selected commentaries, you are at their mercy. If the scholar in your favorite commentary misses a point, you miss it too. If the scholar has a theological axe to grind, you may mistake a conclusion based on prejudice for a pure and simple exposition of the truth.

The insights of commentaries are too valuable to give up entirely. But the proper time to consult them is *after* you have struggled with the text for a while and have reached a tentative interpretation. A commentary may confirm your insights. It may sound a warning against your going off the deep end with a false interpretation. Or a commentary may point out something crucial that you missed.

Beginning students of the Bible may want to consult a one-volume commentary on the whole Bible such as *Harper's Bible Commentary*, edited by James L. Mays (Harper and Row, 1988) or *The Interpreter's One-Volume Commentary on the Bible*, edited by Charles M. Laymon (Abingdon, 1971). The paperback *Basic Bible Commentary* (Abingdon, twenty-nine volumes, 1994) also offers guidance to beginners in an affordable format.

To dig deeper, you will need to consult a multi-volume critical commentary. I strongly recommend the twelve-volume *New Interpreter's Bible* (Abingdon, 1994–2000), which has been explicitly designed to make biblical scholarship accessible and useful to clergy and laity in the churches. Whenever possible, it is best to consult more than one commentary. No single perspective can capture all of the meanings and significance in a particular biblical book or passage.

Bible Teacher Kit (Abingdon, 1994) is a new resource designed for teachers of the Bible. The kit is bound in a three-ring binder that will allow the teacher to personally organize and add to the material. Included in the kit are articles on various sections and books of the Bible, maps of Bible lands (ten one-color maps that can be photocopied and eight 20" by 32" full-color maps), charts, a glossary of names and terms from the Bible, a timeline of kings and prophets, and a video of Bible lands.

When all is said and done about tools for Bible study, the Bible is still the most important resource. No matter how useful secondary sources can be, it would be a great mistake to let reference tools absorb more attention than the Bible itself. So use the tools to help unlock the riches of Scripture but keep clearly in mind which book is the real treasure chest.

This section is adapted from an article, "Basic Tools for Bible Study," by Jack Keller, Reference Products Senior Editor for Abingdon Press. The article appeared in *Leader in the Church School Today*, Fall 1988; pages 20–22. Copyright © 1988 by Graded Press.

4

**Isaiah 40;
42:9-11;
43:18-21;
44:21-22;
46:8-11; 51:1-6**

Do Not Fear, for I Have Redeemed You

LEARNING MENU

Based on your knowledge of class members, their interests and needs, and the learning approaches that work best, choose at least one learning exercise from each of the three following Dimensions. Spend approximately one-third of your class time working on a Dimension 1 activity. Remember, however, that approximately two-thirds of class time should be spent on Dimensions 2 and 3.

Dimension 1:
What Does the Bible Say?

(A) Open with a time of worship.

- Read the information in the "Additional Bible Helps," on "Eagles in the Bible" (page 22). This powerful image of being raised up by God on eagle's wings inspired the contemporary hymn writer Michael Joncas. The Isaiah passage, 4:31, is not the only place in the Bible where this image is found. This image is also used in Exodus 19:4 where Moses encounters God at Mount Sinai.
- Share some of the information from "Eagles in the Bible" with class members; then sing together "On Eagle's Wings," *The United Methodist Hymnal*, 143.

(B) Answer the Dimension 1 questions.

- Remind class members that they can enhance their Bible study by reading and answering these questions prior to class time. If class members have already worked through the questions in Dimension 1, spend approximately ten to fifteen minutes sharing and discussing their answers to the questions. If they have not worked through the questions prior to class time, provide a few minutes for reading the suggested biblical text, along with the questions, either individually or in small teams.
- Discussion of Dimension 1 questions might evoke the following responses:
1. According to Isaiah 40:3-5, a highway will run straight through the desert separating Babylonia and Jerusalem. An enormous leveling process will both raise valleys and reduce mountains, resulting in flat terrain. Upon this highway, God's glory will be revealed for all the nations to see. Later in the Second Isaiah chapters, the prophet will return to the theme of transformed wilderness, proclaiming that the desert will become well-watered, fertile land for Israel to pass through (Isaiah 41:17-20; 43:18-21; 55:12-13).
2. The implied answer to the rhetorical questions in verse 12 is "Yahweh" or the Lord God. Only Israel's God is capable of performing these deeds. Indeed, as these questions further imply, Yahweh is able to perform

these deeds because God is the Creator of heaven and earth.

3. The implied answer to the rhetorical questions in verses 13-14 is "no one." God has no need to consult others for enlightenment, or for instruction in justice, knowledge, and understanding. God's justice, knowledge, and understanding are unrivaled, either by human beings or by other deities.

4. Yahweh's power and sovereignty are a major focus of the Second Isaiah writings (Chapters 40–55). Isaiah 40:18-20 points to the folly of comparing idols (the products of human hands) to God. Verses 22-24 assert the superiority of Yahweh, who rules and regards the earth from heaven, over the earth's rulers, who are likened to short-lived plants. Verses 30-31 assert both God's strength and God's ability to strengthen human beings.

(C) Paraphrase important assertions in Isaiah 40.

If you would like to add a musical dimension to this learning option, secure a recording of Handel's *Messiah* prior to class time. Bring the recording, along with an appropriate player, to this session.

- For this option, provide class members with Bibles, commentaries, and other Bible resource books; paper, and pencils or pens.
- Divide class members into groups of three to four persons each.
- Ask half the groups to paraphrase what is said in Isaiah 40 about the nations (verses 15-17, 22-24). Ask the other half to paraphrase what is said in Isaiah 40 about God's victory march (verses 3-5, 9-11). When possible, paraphrase with images or sayings that are familiar today.
  —How do you try to describe God's power and majesty?
- Some of these verses will sound very familiar to people who have sung or listened to Handel's *Messiah*. If you have a recording of this masterpiece, play the opening recitative "Comfort ye" and the aria "He shall feed His flock."
- At the end of eight to ten minutes working time, invite a spokesperson from each group to read its paraphrase.
- After any class discussion you could play other recorded inspirations from *Messiah*. Humans have tried various means by which to convey a glimmer of God's majesty. Handel's gift continues to convey God's majesty and to inspire us.

Dimension 2: What Does the Bible Mean?

(D) Compose a response from exile.

- You will need Bibles, paper, and pencils or pens for this activity.
- Divide class members into groups of three or four persons each.
- Ask each group to read the information in the study book, "A Flashback—God's Plan for Israel" and "Trust in God's Promises," pages 32–33. Also if class members have not read the following Scripture passages, give them time to do so now:
  —Isaiah 42:9-11
  —Isaiah 43:18-21
  —Isaiah 46:8-11
- Then ask each group to compose a possible response by the exiles to Second Isaiah's challenge that they return to Jerusalem.
- Remember that not all the exiles would have responded in exactly the same way. Many of these were second-generation exiles; they had never lived in the homeland.
- At the end of eight to ten minutes, ask a spokesperson from each group to report its response or responses.

(E) Analyze one of Second Isaiah's poems.

- You will need Bibles, commentaries, paper, and pencils or pens for your class members to use.
- Divide class participants into pairs.
- Ask a member of each pair to the read the poem in Isaiah 41:17-20 aloud.
- Then ask each pair to review the section in the study book titled, "Preparations for Your Journey With Isaiah: Hebrew Poetry" (page 7).
- Ask each pair to analyze the use in Isaiah 41:17-20 of synonymous, antithetical, and/or synthetic parallelism.
  —How does water imagery function in this poem?
  —What does this poem say about the Lord's control over nature?
  —For what purpose or purposes does God transform the desert?
- At the end of ten minutes, request that a spokesperson for each pair tell some of its findings to the class as a whole.

(F) Illustrate one of Second Isaiah's poems.

- For this activity you will need posterboard or heavy paper, magazines with pictures (including news magazines), scissors, crayons, and markers.

- Ask class members to sit comfortably with eyes closed as you slowly read Isaiah 51:4-6.
- At the end of the reading, divide participants into groups of three or four members each.
- Ask persons in each group to work together on a collage that illustrates these verses. If a literal illustration of the translation snags up a group, encourage them to think of modern paraphrases for some of the images and poetry. Remember that Hebrew poetry, like modern poetry, uses wordplays and words rich with meaning and symbolism.
- At the end of fifteen minutes, ask groups to show their collages to the class as a whole and to display them in the classroom throughout the remainder of their study of the Book of Isaiah.

(G) Join in a hymn of praise to God.

- For the closing of this learning option you will need copies of *The United Methodist Hymnal*.
- Read the following paragraphs or tell the information in them to class members:

  Here and there in the Second Isaiah chapters, we find invitations to join in songs of praise to God. Second Isaiah anticipates a time when all creation, and not just Israel, will join in the joyous chorus.

  According to Isaiah 42:10-12, for example, the sea itself will roar its praise; the desert and its settlements will lift up their voices. Inhabitants of Sela (SEE-luh), a fortress city of Edom (EE-duhm), Israel's enemy, will sing for joy. Isaiah 44:23 commands that the heavens, the earth, the mountains, the forest and every tree in it break forth into singing (see also 49:13). Back in the homeland, desolate Jerusalem is urged to burst into song and to shout (54:1).

- Discuss with your class members these images found in Isaiah.
  - You may want to have class members read aloud the following Scripture passages: 42:10-12; 44:23; 49:13; and 54:1.
  - Where have they heard or seen similar images of creation joining in praise to God?
  - What are some contemporary images of creation and inanimate objects praising God?
- Now give class members hymnals containing the hymn, "All Creatures of Our God and King" (*The United Methodist Hymnal*, 62). In the spirit of Second Isaiah's summons, join together in singing this marvelous hymn of praise.

(H) "Cry out!"

Part One:
- Share the following information with class members:
  In Isaiah 40:6, an anonymous voice utters a discouraged response to the summons, "Cry out!" asking, "What shall I cry?"

  When a voice commands, "Cry out!" a sole speaker responds, "What shall I cry?" The identity of this sole speaker is in doubt. If the Second Isaiah corpus existed for a time independent of the Isaian traditions in Isaiah 1–39, the audience likely identified the speaker as Second Isaiah. But if Isaiah 40–55 never existed independent of the Isaian traditions (note that, unlike Isaiah 1:1 and 2:1, Chapter 40 begins without its own superscription [see Isaiah 1:1] and without explicitly identifying the speaker in verse 3, or the two speakers in verse 6), we cannot simply assume that readers of Isaiah's vision, in its final form at least, would have attributed the question, "What shall I cry?" to Second Isaiah. Perhaps they identified the speaker as the same prophet who, in Chapter 6, received his commission to prophesy, that is, Jerusalem Isaiah. After all, from the perspective of readers of Isaiah 1–39, Isaiah's vision had already extended to periods far beyond his own lifetime.

- Then ask class members to divide into four small groups. Recruit a reader from each group. Ask the reader to read aloud Isaiah 40:6-8.
- Ask the small groups to discuss the following questions:
  - Why is the speaker discouraged?
  - What effect has his use of plant imagery on the impact of his message?
- The question, "What shall I cry?" reveals the prophet's discouragement over the brevity of human life. Just as grass springs up quickly and flowers blossom, only to fade away rapidly, so human beings wither and die after only a short period of life. (We might crudely characterize the speaker's response as follows: "What's the use?") Through his use of plant imagery, the poet invites his audience to view human existence through the metaphorical lens of grass and flowers.

  In ancient Israel's world, where plant life was dependent on seasonal rainfall and quickly vanished once the rains stopped, the metaphor undoubtedly served effectively to underscore both the beauty of human existence and its brevity. The one who answers acknowledges the transience of human life but insists that, by contrast, "the word of our God will stand forever" (40:8b).

Part Two:
- Also ask the small groups to discuss the theory that the Book of Isaiah might have had several authors. Bring in the idea that God's word (by the prophets) continued to be used and quoted. This idea reinforced that God's message would continue to "live."
  - How does this concept of a prophet's words continuing to "live" and inform people sound to you?
  - Have you been inspired by the words found in the Book of Isaiah? If so which ones and when?

(I) Identify modern exiles.

> During the week be reading the newspaper or news magazines for articles about and photographs of refugees.
>
> These pictures may reflect the eastern European political situation or refugee situations in Europe, Asia, and Africa. Collect these news articles to have available in class time for this learning option. Also a world map or a large globe would be helpful in locating these areas of unrest.

- For this learning option you will need large sheets of paper or posterboard and markers.
- Share the following information with class members along with news articles, photographs, and maps.

  Across the world, communities are living in exile. Persons flee in order to avoid enemy troops. They must abandon their land on account of drought and famine. They may be forced to leave their homeland in order to find work or to escape oppression and poverty.

  Exile can be emotional, as well as physical. The middle-aged businesswoman or businessman who loses a long-held job may experience feelings of exile. A mother whose children have grown and left home may feel exiled from their lives. Homeless families undoubtedly wrestle with feelings of exile.
- Divide class members into small groups.
- Each group should appoint a "scribe" to record its responses.
- Ask each group to identify three contemporary situations of exile.
- Then ask the groups to discuss these questions:
  —How might Second Isaiah have responded to these modern-day experiences of exile?
  —Identify two concrete ways in which we, as Christians, can respond to others' experiences of exile. Locally, within the congregation, globally?
  —When have you personally felt in exile? Can this personal experience help inform your response to others?
- Next ask the groups to share their ideas with the whole class.
- If class members seem really interested in leaning more about contemporary exile situations, and thus helping Isaiah's words continue to "live," write or call Service Center, General Board of Global Ministries—7820 Reading Road, Cincinnati, Ohio 45222-1800; phone (513) 761-2100—for a catalog of the mission resources for The United Methodist Church.

(J) Respond to God's summons in your life.

- Review the information from the study book section "Second Isaiah's Invitation" (page 35) with class members.
- Then ask them to close their eyes, get in a comfortable sitting position, and listen intently as you read Isaiah 43:16-21. Suggest that they keep their eyes closed for a few moments after the reading has ended.
- After the reading, allow people time to reflect on the Scripture passage. Then ask that these questions be reflected on silently (allow several minutes of silence between each question):
  —What "new thing" would I wish God to begin in my life?
  —How can I, with God's help, make a way through my own wilderness experiences?
  —When in my daily routine can I make time to praise God?
- To close today's session, ask people to end their reflections with a silent prayer asking God to hear their thoughts and to help them respond to God's invitation through the words of Second Isaiah.

(K) Close with prayer.

- Ask class members to sit quietly with their eyes closed as you read aloud Isaiah 40:28-31. When you have finished reading, allow a few moments for class members to reflect upon what they have heard.
- Lead class members in the following prayer. Ask them to repeat each line after you:

  —"Lord, strengthen me so that I can soar like the eagles and enjoy the flight!
  —"Lord, empower me so that I can run when I must and not be weary.
  —"Lord, sustain me so that I can walk through my most mundane tasks and not faint.
  —"Lord, when I grow weary, help me to be your agent in taking care of me. Amen."

Additional Bible Helps

The Prophet—Second Isaiah

The poetry of Second Isaiah takes its place among the finest literature in our Bible. Obviously, its anonymous author possessed extraordinary poetic gifts. But he was also an astute and sensitive student of human nature. He recognized the fear—including the fear to hope—that plagued his exilic community. He knew their sorrows and their complacencies. He was aware of human reluctance to step out into unknown situations.

In presenting God's liberating message to the Babylonian exiles, Second Isaiah spoke of God's "new thing." His words painted portraits of a marvelous age of forgiveness, salvation, peace, and prosperity. But he also recognized the importance of reminding people where they came from. Second Isaiah's new thing evoked memories of God's past acts on Israel's behalf, notably the Exodus from Egyptian slavery. This decisive event in Israel's history functioned to illumine God's imminent redemption of Israel.

We should not think that Second Isaiah received knowledge of Israel's religious traditions effortlessly. God's prophets were not parrots. They had the hard task of translating God's messages to their audiences in the most compelling ways possible. While we do not know Second Isaiah's name, we can be sure that a significant portion of his time in exile was spent mastering the religious traditions of his people. He was able to serve effectively as God's prophet when summoned because he had prepared himself.

We too are called to be God's servants and prophets in a world filled with despair, fear, fragile hopes, and uncertainty. In order to fulfill those roles, we too must prepare ourselves. Certainly, we should tend to our spiritual growth, since the closer our relationship with God, the greater our ability to hear and respond to God's summons. Yet we, like the anonymous exilic prophet, need also to familiarize ourselves with our religious heritage. When we are firmly rooted in our faith, we are more likely to know the answer to the question, "What shall I cry?" Yes, grass withers and flowers fade. But "the word of our God will stand forever."

Eagles in the Bible

The eagle is mentioned thirty-four times in the Bible (*Strong's Concordance of the Bible*; Abingdon, 1980). As Americans we may think that only we have eagles, since the bald eagle is our national emblem. However, the eagle has been impressing people with its majesty and swift movements at least since biblical times. Old Testament writers considered this magnificent creature the monarch of the birds. And the eagle was seen in many visions of these early prophets. Ezekiel's four-faced cherubim had the face of an eagle (Ezekiel 1:10; 10:14). Daniel portrayed the Babylonian kingdom by combining the noblest beast with noblest bird—a lion with eagles' wings (Daniel 7:2-4a) (*The Interpreter's Dictionary of the Bible*, Volume E–J; Abingdon Press, 1962; page 1). Therefore, we should not be surprised that the prophet, "Second Isaiah," uses the image of eagles' wings with which to soar the soon-to-be-liberated people.

Who Was Cyrus of Persia?

In 540 B.C. Cyrus (SIGH-ruhs) controlled a vast empire, extending from the Persian Gulf to the Aegean Sea. He had been politically and militarily very successful. In the year 539 B.C. the Persians and Babylonians fought a great battle at Opis on the Tigris River. The Persians won, and serious Babylonian resistance came to an end.

Cyrus's account of his Babylonian triumph is recorded on the famous Cyrus Cylinder—an inscription written on a clay barrel.

The Cyrus Cylinder contains an account of Cyrus's triumph over Babylonia.

The account begins with a condemnation of Nabonidus (nab-uh-NIGH-duhs) for ignoring the temple of Marduk and for subjecting the Bablylonian people to slave labor. Seeing the ruin of Babylonia, Marduk showed mercy. The account goes on to say that Marduk selected Cyrus to march against Babylon "going at his side like a real friend," for Marduk was pleased with Cyrus's kind treatment of his subjects. It was reported that Cyrus was allowed to enter Babylon "without any battle" and was greeted with great warmth. Cyrus boasts of abolishing forced labor, improving housing conditions, and enjoying the affection of the people. He returned sacred images to the peoples from whom they had been taken and rebuilt their sanctuaries. He gathered together foreign exiles and returned them to their homelands.

This of course is the victor's story. Nevertheless, in contrast to other conquerors, especially the Assyrians and the Babylonians, Cyrus was extraordinarily benevolent and humane. He has been called one of the most enlightened rulers in human history.

So began the great Persian Empire. It is against the background of these momentous international developments, which sent a wave of expectancy throughout the ancient world, that we must understand the prophecy of Second Isaiah. (From *The Living World of the Old Testament*, by Bernhard W. Anderson; Longman, 1966; pages 397–99.)

5

Isaiah 52–54; other selected verses

DAUGHTER ZION AND THE SERVANT OF THE LORD

Daughter Zion
(Isaiah 40:2-9; 49:14-26; 51:17–52:10; 54:1-17)

The Servant of the Lord
(Isaiah 42:1-4; 49:1-6; 50:4-9; 52:13–53:12)

LEARNING MENU

Based on your knowledge of the interests and needs of class members, as well as the learning approaches that work best with your class, choose one activity from each of the three following Dimensions. Spend approximately one-third of the session working on a Dimension 1 exercise. Remember, however, that approximately two-thirds of class time should be spent on activities in Dimensions 2 and 3.

Dimension 1:
What Does the Bible Say?

(A) Open with worship.

Share Lady Zion's experiences.
- Ask class members to sit quietly with eyes closed. Explain that the Book of Lamentations, the subject of a later lesson in the study book, draws from women's

experiences in order to portray Jerusalem's plight in the aftermath of "her" destruction by the Babylonians in 587 B.C.
- In a solemn tone, read Lamentations 2:13-19.
- Turn from this depiction of Jerusalem's predicament to Isaiah 52 and read verses 1-2 and 7-10, descriptions of the imminent reversal of Jerusalem's tragic circumstances.
- When you have finished reading, allow a few moments for reflection.
- These two readings should set an appropriate tone for your class time. If you would like to follow-up the reading and reflection time with a question, ask: How does the poetic technique of personifying Jerusalem as a woman affect your understanding of her experiences? (Read the section in "Additional Bible Helps," "Jerusalem Personified as a Woman," page 27, for additional insights.)

(B) Answer the Dimension 1 questions.

- Remind class members that reading the biblical texts and answering Dimension 1 questions prior to class time enhances their Bible study. If they have already worked through the questions, spend ten to fifteen minutes sharing and discussing their answers.
- If they have not yet answered the Dimension 1 ques-

tions, divide your class into two groups. Assign one group the Daughter Zion questions and one group the Servant of the Lord questions. Allow the groups a few minutes to read the questions, along with the relevant biblical texts. Then share the groups' insights with the whole class.

● Discussion of Dimension 1 questions might evoke the following comments:

Daughter Zion

1. Twin imperatives urge Jerusalem, "Awake, awake." (The use of twin imperatives is characteristic of Second Isaiah's literary style.) Captive Daughter Zion sits in a stupor of despair and desolation, down in the dust, with bonds around her neck. But now, the prophet insists, her bondage has ended. It is time once again for her to put on beautiful garments and ascend her throne. No longer shall this holy city be entered by the uncircumcised and the unclean (her enemies).

   The messenger proclaims to Zion words of peace, good news, and salvation. Her sentinels (watchmen), catching sight of God's procession toward Jerusalem, break into songs of joy. But more than human voices join the chorus. Jerusalem's very ruins join in celebrating the marvelous things that the Lord is about to do on Zion's behalf and before the nations.

2. Isaiah 54:1-3 describes the return of Jerusalem's children from exile. So numerous are they that she will have to stretch out her "tent" in order to contain them all. Isaiah 54:4-10 speaks of God's desire to be reconciled with his wife, Jerusalem. The reference to "the disgrace of your widowhood" (verse 4) does not mean that Yahweh, her husband, has died. In this context, *widowhood* describes the predicament of a once-married woman who has lost her (male) protector and, having no others (a mature son), stands in need of both financial provision and legal protection. Reconciliation with her husband means the return of her protector and the end to her present, vulnerable status.

   God swears never again to be angry with or to rebuke Zion. The text likens God's oath to the divine promise to Noah (Genesis 8:21 and 9:9-17) never again to destroy the earth by flood.

The Servant of the Lord

1. God proclaims that his servant, though disfigured, shall prosper and be exalted, to the astonishment of the nations.

2. The unidentified speakers in Isaiah 53:4-6 assert that the servant has suffered on their behalf, for the Lord has placed their iniquity on him. Given the references to "many nations" and "kings" in 52:15, it is reasonable to conclude that these speakers represent peoples other than Israel alone. Hence, these verses seek to explain, at least in part, the reason for Israel's suffering, presenting it as purposeful within God's plan for Israel and the nations.

In bearing the iniquities of others, the righteous servant fulfills his own God-given role, including extending Yahweh's righteousness into the world.

Dimension 2:
What Does the Bible Mean?

(C) Identify responses to destruction.

Second Isaiah offers a variety of responses to complaints about the tragedy of 587 B.C. and its aftermath. (For more information on the fall of Jerusalem, see the "Additional Bible Helps," "Jerusalem, More Than a Symbol," page 27.) You may want to summarize and share information about the incorporation of Jerusalem. This knowledge will help them to better understand the dual devastation felt with Jerusalem's destruction in 587.

● Divide class members into three groups; provide each group with large sheets of paper and markers. Give each group their Scripture assignments.

Group One:
   —Isaiah 40:27-31; 41:11-13; 43:14; 44:21-22
Group Two:
   —Isaiah 45:14; 48:17-19; 49:14-18
Group Three:
   —Isaiah 53:10-12; 54:4-8; 55:12-13

● Ask each group to read its assigned texts and to identify the argument by which Second Isaiah seeks to respond to the exiles' complaints about their past and present predicaments and to urge their return to Jerusalem.

● Group discussions might evoke the following responses:
Group One:
In Isaiah 40:27-31, the prophet claims to quote the exiles' words: "My way is hidden from the LORD, / and my right is disregarded by my God." Second Isaiah counters that God is neither absent nor too weary to respond, possesses unrivaled understanding, and can strengthen the exiles, even in their exhaustion.

Isaiah 41:11-13 reassures the exiles that they need not fear their enemies, since God promises to help them. See also Isaiah 43:14, where the Lord promises that for Israel's sake, the Babylonians will themselves experience defeat and lamentation.

Prior to 587 B.C., Yahweh's prophets identified the sins of Judah's inhabitants and warned that the penalty for these sins would be the collapse of Judah and Jerusalem's destruction. In Isaiah 44:21-22, God solves the problem of Israel's sinfulness by offering the exiles a new beginning, proclaiming that Israel's past sins have been swept away.
Group Two:
The Judeans experienced the humiliation of defeat by foreigners. Isaiah 45:14 promises, however, that mighty nations shall soon bring their wealth to Israel, acknowl-

edging the unrivaled sovereignty of Yahweh, Israel's God.

God did not delight in punishing sinful Israel. In 48:17-19, Yahweh—Israel's teacher and leader—expresses regret that Israel failed to heed God's commandments. Had they done so, they would have averted their tragic past, enjoying abundant prosperity and unlimited offspring.

In 49:14-18, Jerusalem complains that the Lord has abandoned her. But God disavows that possibility, promising that she shall be rebuilt and her children returned to her.

Group Three:

Second Isaiah reinterprets Israel's travail (53:10-12). The Lord's servant (Israel) has indeed suffered, but "his" suffering was part of God's plan. "He" shall see his offspring and prosper. Moreover, his grief brings righteousness to others, on whose behalf he has suffered.

In Isaiah 54:4-8, Second Isaiah reinterprets Israel's punishment. True, Jerusalem has endured the shame and disgrace of abandonment. But Yahweh downplays the severity of God's past anger, seeks reconciliation with "his" wife, and promises her everlasting love.

Second Isaiah encourages the exiles' return to Jerusalem by promising that their procession will be a glorious event, celebrated by the mountains and hills they pass along the way, as trees clap their hands (Isaiah 55:12-13).

- When the groups have finished discussing their texts, reconvene the class, inviting a person from each group to report its findings to the class as a whole.
- You may want to ask these questions of class members:
  —Do you see any common themes within these Scripture passages? If so, what?
  —Were you surprised by any of the images you read? Explain.

(D) Create a collage.

- For this activity you will need posterboard or large sheets of paper, magazines (including news magazines), scissors, glue, and markers.
- Ask class members to sit comfortably with eyes closed as you read Isaiah 49:19-23 slowly.
- At the end of the reading, divide class members into groups of three or four members each.
- Ask persons in each group to work together on a collage that depicts Isaiah 49:19-23, the return of Lady Zion's children. This collage might contain pictures drawn or cut from magazines, words that convey major components of the Scripture passage, and colors that help interpret emotions.
- At the end of fifteen minutes, ask groups to share their collages with the whole class and to display them in the classroom throughout the remainder of their work in the Book of Isaiah.

(E) Look for female imagery in Second Isaiah.

Metaphors invite us to perceive something through terms that are suggestive of something else. Second Isaiah's Lady Zion metaphors describe the city's past, present, and future using language drawn from women's experiences.

- Divide class members into three groups. Provide each group with paper and pencils or pens.
- You may need to have selected some Scripture passages to offer as examples. The passages used in today's lesson would be appropriate: Isaiah 49:14-26; 51:17-23; 54:1-17. Encourage your class members to draw upon other Scripture passages used in previous lessons or those passages read during their daily Scripture reading.
- Write the following questions on the chalkboard or on a large sheet of paper. Ask each group to address these questions:
  —Have you previously noticed biblical female imagery for Jerusalem? If so, where?
  —Are these images helpful communicators for the biblical city? Why, or why not?
  —How might you describe your local city, town, or community?
  —What stereotypical roles, experiences, and ideas about women are highlighted in Second Isaiah's Lady Zion poems? (For example: motherhood, devotion to one's children.)
  —What other examples of biblical personification come to mind?
- At the end of ten minutes, invite a spokesperson from each group to report its findings to the entire class.

(F) Analyze a poem.

Remind participants that careful reading of Second Isaiah's poems brings to light features that may otherwise go unnoticed.

- Review "Preparations for Your Journey With Isaiah: Hebrew Poetry" (page 7 in the study book).
- Divide class members into three or four working groups. Provide each group with paper and pencils or pens.
- Invite one member of each group to read aloud Isaiah 49:1-7, the third servant poem.
- After the reading, ask each group to address the following questions. (Write them on a large sheet of newsprint or other paper before this session so groups can consult them as they work.)
  —Does the poem contain examples of synonymous parallelism? If so, where?
  —Does the poem contain lines exhibiting synthetic parallelism? If so, where?
  —What types of poetic imagery (light imagery in verse 6) does the poet use?
  —What are the effects of the quotations (verses 3, 4, 6,

7) incorporated into the poem? Do they, for example, strengthen your sense of the poem's authority?

—What, based on this poem, is your impression of the servant?

● At the end of ten to twelve minutes, invite a representative from each group to report its insights to the class as a whole.

Dimension 3:
What Does the Bible Mean to Us?

(G) Argue against God's words.

In times of distress and discontent, we may respond to affirmations about God's sustaining love and power with disbelief and even anger. In the Old Testament, no less than Abraham, Moses, and Job dared to express frustration and anger toward God in troubling times; and they were not rebuked for doing so.

● Divide class members into two or four groups. (One group to work with each passage or two groups to work with each passage.) Give each group paper and pencils or pens.

● Ask each group to argue against the perspective advanced by Second Isaiah in one of these two texts: Isaiah 48:6-11; Isaiah 51:12-16. Tell the groups that they are arguing as if they are the chosen people of Israel who have been "blessed" by God. Then ask one group member to be the prophet while the other members are those enslaved in Babylonia. Enjoy the creativity of your class members as they converse with the prophet.

● At the end of ten minutes, invite a representative from each group to share its arguments with the class as a whole.

● At this point you may want to share with class members information found in the "Additional Bible Helps" entitled "Second Isaiah's Strategies" (see next column).

● You may also wish to have a whole class discussion about how we as Christians hear and believe in God's love and concern in our times of struggle and pain.

(H) Consider the relationship between Israel and its God.

● Ask class members to sit quietly with eyes closed while you read Isaiah 44:24-28. Allow additional quiet time at the end of the reading for individual reflection.

● After the reading, divide class members into conversation groups of two or three persons. Ask them, in light of Isaiah 44:24-28, to consider the following questions:
—What images came to mind as this Scripture passage was being read?

—What do these verses tell us about God?
—What do these verses tell us about God's attitude toward Israel?
—What do these verses suggest about our relationship with God?

● Ask each group to share several of its reflections with the class as a whole.

(I) Consider the relationship between the servant and God.

● In preparation, read "God's Servant Is Israel" in "Additional Bible Helps, " page 27.

● Ask class members to listen quietly and close their eyes as you read Isaiah 49:1-7. Allow additional time for personal reflection at the end of the reading.

● After the reading, divide class members into conversation groups of two to four persons.

● Ask them, in light of Isaiah 49:1-7, to discuss the following questions:
—What images came to mind as you heard this Scripture passage being read?
—What do these verses tell us about God?
—What do these verses tell us about the servant's role?
—What do these verses tell us about God's attitude toward the nations?
—What do these verses suggest about God's relationship with us and our relationship with the world?

● After the groups have had a time for discussion, ask each group to share several of its reflections with the class as a whole.

● At this time you may want to share additional information from the "Additional Bible Helps: God's Servant Is Israel."

(J) Close with worship.

● Conclude this session by reading Isaiah 43:1-2 to class members. Then ask everyone to join in singing the hymn "How Firm a Foundation," *The United Methodist Hymnal*, 529. If hymnals are not available for your whole class, you could read aloud stanzas 3 and 4 of the hymn. These two verses were inspired by Isaiah 43:1-2.

Additional Bible Helps

Second Isaiah's Strategies
On first reading, we may be tempted to conclude that Second Isaiah's oracles reached an enthusiastic audience, ready and willing to return to Jerusalem at God's command. Careful analysis reveals, however, that the prophet felt compelled to use a variety of theological arguments and literary strategies in order to convince his audience that

1. they had not been abandoned by their God;

2. their God was the sovereign Creator of the world and Ruler of history;

3. God had swept their sins away;

4. Jerusalem was on the verge of a great transformation, such that her desolate environs would become "like the garden of the Lord" (Isaiah 51:3);

5. their suffering had redemptive significance both for Israel and others; and

6. the nations would acknowledge and celebrate Yahweh while bringing their wealth to glorified Zion.

We should not wonder that Second Isaiah's "good news" was hard to hear for at least many of the exiles. Did not their current circumstances point to precisely the opposite of Second Isaiah's promises? The prophet persevered, nonetheless, rooting his message deep in Israel's most ancient and esteemed traditions (the Exodus), yet announcing a new stage in the history of Israel's relationship with its God, a stage integral to Yahweh's ongoing plan for Israel and the nations.

Both the Daughter Zion poems, and the Servant of the Lord passages, function to further the prophet's goal. These passages personalize and intensify God's relationship to Jerusalem and her inhabitants on the one hand and reinterpret the meaning of Israel's suffering for its ongoing life and for the nations on the other. So powerful were these poems that subsequent generations of Jews, including the earliest Christians and their descendants in the faith, have returned to them again and again for the light they shed on God's ongoing plan for the faithful.

Jerusalem Personified as a Woman

When Second Isaiah personified Jerusalem as a woman, he was not creating a new poetic image. To the contrary, cities appear in the guise of women not only in other biblical books, but also in the writings of some of Israel's ancient Near Eastern neighbors. Tikva Frymer-Kensky, a specialist in ancient Near Eastern literature, points out that personifying cities as women made good psychological sense: "the city contains the populace within her walls, nurtures it, provides for it, and defends it" (*In the Wake of the Goddesses: Women, Culture, and the Biblical Transformation of the Pagan Myth*; The Free Press, 1992; page 172).

God's Servant Is Israel

In his textbook, *Understanding the Old Testament*, noted biblical scholar and theologian Bernard W. Anderson summarizes this view of Israel as God's servant.

"So far, it would seem that Second Isaiah identifies the Servant with the covenant community of Israel. Plumbing the meaning of the intense suffering occasioned by the fall of the nation, he affirms that in 'the furnace of affliction' (48:10) Yahweh has refined the people for greater service. In one sense, the national catastrophe came as God's judg-ment upon Israel's foolishness and disobedience, just as prophets of the past had prophesied (see 42:18-25). But, according to this prophet, Israel has paid the penalty for the past, and is now accepted and renewed by Yahweh's freely offered forgiveness (40:1-2; 43:22–44:5). As iron is tempered by fire and shaped on the anvil, so Yahweh re-creates the people through sufferings so that they may be a more effective instrument of the divine purpose in history" (*Understanding the Old Testament*, 4th edition; Prentice-Hall, 1986; page 491).

Jerusalem, More Than a Symbol

This holy city outranks all other cities of the Bible in prominence and wealth of sacred associations. Jerusalem is thought to be the chief city in Palestine, sacred to the Jews and to the Christians to this day as the "city of the great King."

Under one name or another Jerusalem appears in about two thirds of the books in the Old Testament and in about half of the books in the New Testament. This city is also the third most holy city of Islam to the Muslims (*The Interpreter's Dictionary of the Bible*, Volume E–J; Abingdon Press, 1982; page 843).

The circumstances that surrounded Jerusalem's inclusion into the tribal territory of Israel are of importance as we study biblical events. In a strategic political move, the brilliant military commander David made his bid for power by wisely choosing a place for his capital that was neither "northern" nor "southern." He selected the neutral site of Jerusalem on the boundary of the northern and southern tribes. In this new capital, the administration of law, which previously had been vested in tribal "judges," was taken over by the king himself. King David appointed some of these judges to royal offices that would serve under his direction.

The administration of law was not enough to capture the allegiance of all Israel. David also "had to demonstrate that his political innovations would not sweep away Israel's sacred heritage, but bring it to glorious fulfillment. So one of his shrewdest acts was to rescue the Ark of the Covenant from the place of oblivion . . . Shiloh and to bring it to Jerusalem with great pomp and ceremony [1 Samuel 6]. . . . With the Ark stationed in a 'tent' in Jerusalem, the city of David also became 'Zion, City of God,' for Yahweh's presence once again 'tabernacled' in the midst of Israel" (*Understanding the Old Testament*, 4th edition; page 224).

Therefore, we must bear in mind the importance centered in the control of Jerusalem. When Jerusalem was destroyed in 587, not only was a capital city raided and put under hostile rule, but Yahweh's sacred "tent" was also destroyed. The people of Israel not only lost their main city of commerce, but this religious center was no longer theirs.

6 OLD PROBLEMS... NEW EARTH

Isaiah 58–59; 65

Dimension 1:
What Does the Bible Say?

(A) Begin with a time for worship.

● As you begin your study of this final lesson on Isaiah, you will have upmost in your mind the vision of the new earth that Isaiah proclaims. A recommended hymn to call class members together and begin your session is "Marching to Zion," *The United Methodist Hymnal*, 733.

(B) Discuss Dimension 1 questions.

Remind class members that they will enhance their Bible study if they read and answer these questions before the class session. If persons have worked through the questions in Dimension 1 prior to class time, spend time sharing and discussing their answers. If they have not worked through the questions, provide a few minutes for reading the biblical texts and the questions, either individually or in teams.

● Discussion questions might evoke the following responses:

1. In Isaiah 58:2-5, God questions Israel's incentive for its religious practices. True, the people have *acted as if* they were "a nation that practiced righteousness." They engage in acts of worship and fasting. But they become angry when their fasts do not "work," that is, when they fail to produce the desired results (verse 3). Yahweh responds by charging that such acts are self-motivated. Those who fast turn right around and oppress their employees; they are quarrelsome, arrogant, and selfish. Fasting and external acts of humility mean nothing unless they grow out of genuine righteousness.

2. From the perspective of the Third Isaiah community, justice is perverted by those who shed innocent blood, oppress the vulnerable, and pervert the legal system. On account of their misdeeds, "justice is turned back, / and righteousness stands at a distance" (59:14a).

3. For the sake of the Lord's servants, God will not destroy all Israel. Yahweh's servants will eat, drink, rejoice, and prosper. Those who perpetuate the sins of Israel's past,

by contrast, shall hunger, thirst, and be put to shame.

4. According to Isaiah 65:17-25, Jerusalem and its right-eous inhabitants shall know great joy. The city will thrive. Infant mortality will become a thing of the past. Indeed, persons will live for more than one hundred years! The land will be fruitful, and animals—both predators and their former prey—will dwell together in peace.

(C) Identify God's moral mandates.

- You will need to provide class members with paper and pens or pencils to use during this learning option.
- Ask class members to listen carefully as you read Isaiah 58:6-14. Ask them to write on their piece of paper what these verses say that God requires of the people.
- After you finish reading, record on the chalkboard or on a large piece of paper a list of God's moral mandates, compiled from the class members' lists of what God requires of the people.
- When you have finished writing the list, turn to Matthew 25:31-46, and read it aloud. Again ask class members to take notes as you read. What mandates appearing in Isaiah 58 also appear in the Matthew passage?
- Check off on the list those mandates common to both texts.
- Then discuss these ideas with class members:
  —Where do you hear the strongest "echo" of the Old Testament mandate in the New Testament?
  —Where do the mandates differ?
  —Do any of these differences raise questions? If so, why?
  —Which set of mandates speak more to you? Why?

Dimension 2: What Does the Bible Mean?

(D) Find the figurative language in Third Isaiah's poetry.

- For this activity you will need various colors of construction paper, crayons, magazines, and markers.
- Divide class members into three or four groups; provide each group with art supplies.
- Ask a member of each group to read aloud, verse by verse, Isaiah 59:1-15.
- Make a list of the poem's uses of figurative language. It contains many metaphors ("they hatch adders' eggs"; verse 5); similes ("we all growl like bears; like doves we moan mournfully"; verse 11); personification ("for truth stumbles in the public square"; verse 14b).
- After each group has compiled its list, ask group members to discuss the impact of these uses of figurative lan-

guage on the poem's meaning. Ask members, or a group-appointed artist, to illustrate one of the images that is used. Does the figurative language make the poem's statements more vivid and memorable?
- At the end of ten minutes, invite a representative from each group to tell several of its observations and show its drawings to the whole class.

(E) Picture a new earth.

- For this activity you will need magazines (including news magazines), posterboard, scissors, glue, and markers.
- Divide class members into three or four groups. Ask each group to make a collage showing God's new heavens and new earth as described in Isaiah 65:17-25. If the passage seems too long to illustrate in its entirety, then the groups could choose a verse or two of the longer passage that seems to really speak to them as an important component in the new heavens and new earth view.
- At the end of fifteen minutes, invite each group to show and explain its artwork to the whole class.
- Encourage groups to display their collages in the classroom.

(F) Make a word collage.

- You will need posterboard or large sheets of paper and markers for this option.
- Divide class members into three groups; provide each group with paper and markers.
- Assign each group a portion of Isaiah 65:
  Group One can focus on verses 1-7;
  Group Two can focus on verses 8-16;.
  Group Three can focus on verses 17-25.
- Ask someone from each group to read its verses aloud.
- After the reading, each group should ask the following questions of its text. As the groups work through the questions have them make word collages (one per group) using key words from their answers.
  —What do these verses tell us about God?
  —What do they tell us about human beings?
  —What do they tell us about our relationships with God?
  —What, according to this text, is God's will for human communities?
- At the end of ten minutes, invite a person from each group to show its word collage to the class and tell insights this activity may have prompted.

(G) Consider the servants' predicament.

The Third Isaiah community regarded itself as the true disciples of Second Isaiah, the "servants of the Lord." Yet many of Second Isaiah's prophecies failed to materialize following the return from Babylonian exile to Palestine in 538 B.C.

- For this learning option you will need several Bible translations, Bible commentaries, paper, and pencils or pens.
- Divide class members into small groups. See that each group has several different Bible translations, a Bible commentary, paper, and pencils or pens.
- Ask each group to identify two prophecies of Second Isaiah that, from the postexilic community's perspective, were as yet unfulfilled. (In addition to considering the three chapters we have studied in this lesson, also use Isaiah 64:9-12.) As the groups consider these questions, ask them to jot down the Scripture reference they were working with:
  —What were the effects of these unfulfilled prophecies upon the "servants of the Lord"?
  —The Third Isaiah group witnessed the reemergence of old sins in its midst. Identify two problems that plagued their postexilic community. What do you think were the effects of these sins upon the "servants of the Lord"?
  —How did the prophecy of a "new heavens and a new earth" speak to their disappointments and problems?

Dimension 3:
What Does the Bible Mean to Us?

(H) Compare leaders then with now.

Isaiah's vision began (in Chapter 1) with scathing indictments of Israel's leadership. The poems of Third Isaiah return to this theme, charging the postexilic community's leaders with similar sins.
- Be sure to have a variety of Bible translations available for class members to use. You will need a large sheet of paper or chalkboard upon which to record the class members' insights.
- Return to Isaiah 1. Ask one class member to read verses 10-17 aloud. Ask the rest of your class members to follow along in their Bibles.
- Then ask another class member to read aloud Isaiah 59:1-8.
- At the conclusion of both readings, ask persons to identify similarities between the charges levied in Isaiah 1:10-17 and those cited in Isaiah 59:1-8. At this time you may wish to record the class findings on the chalkboard or paper.
- Then ask these questions of your class members:
  —Are any of these charges applicable to contemporary national leadership groups? Why, or why not?
  —How might we "wash [ourselves]; make [ourselves] clean; / remove the evil of [our] doings from before [God's] eyes; / cease to do evil, / learn to do good; / seek justice, / rescue the orphan, / plead for the widow" (1:16-17)?

- Conclude this activity by offering sentence prayers on behalf of our national leaders. Each class member should feel free to contribute a sentence or two to this community prayer or to remain silent in participation.

(I) Choose a fast.

In this learning option class members will explore the rich meaning of the word *fast*.
Part One
- Divide class members into small conversation groups (three to four persons each). Begin with a discussion on *fast*. These questions may help them get started:
  —When you hear the word *fast* in a biblical context what do you think of?
  —During Lent (the forty days that precede Easter) or any other time have any of you practiced fasting? What was your experience like?
- Ask a class member to read aloud Isaiah 58:6-9a. In the small groups, discuss what kind of fast God requires. (The *fast* God chooses consists of acts of justice and righteousness, not empty displays of piety. Those who would truly serve Yahweh oppose acts of injustice, liberate the oppressed, feed the hungry, house and clothe the homeless, and do not avoid family obligations.)
  —How does Isaiah's interpretation of *fast* differ from our modern understanding?
Part Two
- Read aloud Isaiah 58:9b-14. Continue with your small groups, and discuss this question:
  —What does the Lord promise to do on behalf of those whose attitudes and actions are pleasing to God? (God will guide Israel and abundantly meet its needs. It shall grow and prosper, its ruined cities and settlements will be rebuilt, and the Lord will exalt Israel, causing it to "ride upon the heights of the earth" [verse 14].)
- Close with a time of silence and prayer. You may choose to use this prayer:
  God of Justice:
  Guide us to choose the fast of justice and freedom;
  give us opportunities to share our bread with the hungry,
  to open our homes to the homeless poor.
  Then help us to see the new dawn as your light breaks forth!

(J) Restore a broken relationship with God.

- You will need an index card or small piece of paper for each class member, plus a pencil or pen for each to use.
- Divide class members into small groups of three or four members each. The number of groups will depend on your total class size.
- Read Isaiah 63:7–64:12 aloud. Then ask the groups these questions:

—How does this section begin (63:7-9)?

—What happens next?

—What is the main historical event that is mentioned?

—Where is the "blame" cast (63:17) regarding the unfaithfulness?

- Share this information with your class: Isaiah 63:7–64:12 contains a lengthy lament by those Israelites who desperately wish to restore their relationship with God. "Do not be exceedingly angry, O LORD," they pray (64:9). Recalling the punishments of the past (verses 10-11), they ask, "After all this, will you restrain yourself, O LORD? / Will you keep silent, and punish us so severely?" Isaiah 65 contains God's response to their lament.

- Then pose this question to class members: How does the Lord answer the lamenters' complaint that God has fallen silent (Isaiah 65:1-7)? (God flatly refutes Israel's complaint of divine silence. To the contrary, God claims continually to have taken the initiative with Israel, though they have historically refused every overture. Indeed, at least some of the people continue to engage in horrible offenses against the Lord, while daring to assert their superior holiness (verses 3-5). To them, God promises punishment proportionate to their sins (verses 6-7).

- After exploring the Scripture text, ask your groups to discuss this question:

—How are we—our congregation, our denomination, the wider Christian church—like our Israelite ancestors?

- Close this session by passing out an index card to each person for him or her to write out the answer to the following question:

—When has God held out God's hands to you and you were too busy to respond? (Reassure your class members that these answers will not be read aloud.)

- Gather these confessions; destroy them. (You could burn them or just cut them up into very small pieces.) Then read aloud Isaiah 64:8-9, and close by singing "Have Thine Own Way, Lord," *The United Methodist Hymnal*, 382.

(K) Describe your vision for peace.

- For this learning option you will need small slips of paper and pencils or pens, and a container for collecting the paper slips.

- In this learning option you will be hearing some dreams and visions your class members have for the new heaven and the new earth.

- Begin with these words: We have read and heard the prophets from the Book of Isaiah proclaim components of the new creation. Throughout the ages prophets and leaders have spun out their visions for peace and the worship of God. What are your ideas?

- Pass out slips of paper and pencils. Have class members write down their ideas on a slip of paper. Fold these up and put them in a container. Shake up the slips. Pass around the container asking individuals to select one paper (not read) until all are selected.

- Share these "visions" with the whole class in a "popcorn" style. A beginning sentence might be something like this: "We believe that God will continue to be active in creation. Our vision is one of a new creation where . . . [read slip of paper]."

- Close with this prayer: O God, we wait for your new creation. We trust in your wisdom. We believe in your grace. We long to be in closer communion with you! Amen.

(L) Close with worship.

- Participate in a "Canticle of Light and Darkness." (The following Canticle appears on page 205 of *The United Methodist Hymnal*.)

- Write on a large piece of paper or on the chalkboard so that all can see the following class response: "The people who walked in darkness have seen a great light."

- Ask three members of the class to read the following Scripture passages. If you have someone who is comfortable teaching and leading the sung response (1) for this canticle, give it a try. If not, have everyone repeat the response in unison after each Scripture section is read.

Response: "The people who walked in darkness have seen a great light."

Reader One: "We look for light but find darkness, for brightness, but walk in gloom. We grope like those who have no eyes; we stumble at noon as in the twilight."

Response:

Reader Two: "If I say, 'Let only darkness cover me, and the light about me be night,' even the darkness is not dark to you, the night is bright as the day, for darkness is as light with you."

Response:

Reader Three: "Blessed be your name, O God, for ever. You reveal deep and mysterious things; you are light and in you is no darkness. Our darkness is passing away and already the true light is shining."

Response:

Isaiah Over the Years

No other biblical prophetic book spans so many crucial centuries in Israel's history as does the Book of Isaiah. From the Syro-Israelite crisis in 735–733 B.C. to the struggles of postexilic Judaism, Isaiah's vision addressed Israel's condition:

—identifying its sins;

—insisting on Yahweh's justice and righteousness;

—warning of the consequences of transgressions;

—emphasizing Yahweh's ultimate plan for Israel and the nations;

—holding out the possibilities of forgiveness and salvation;

—urging obedience to God's will and trust in Yahweh's power and sovereignty.

When we recognize that Isaiah's vision represents the theological wrestlings and reflections of generations of Israelites and not just the work of a lone individual, its significance for our faith communities grows. Clearly, God's word was not given once and for all in the distant past. The word of the Lord is not static. To the contrary, it must be reclaimed and proclaimed by each generation in response to ever-changing challenges.

Though the Book of Isaiah has an ending, Isaiah's vision remains open. The options it gives us remain options; and as men and women of faith we, no less than the ancient Israelites, must choose whether to travel the path leading to obedience and salvation, or the path of persistent rebellion against God leading ultimately to destruction. Isaiah's vision everywhere urges us to choose God. Choose life!

7

Jeremiah 1:1–4:4

"Now I Have Put My Words in Your Mouth"

Dimension 1:
What Does the Bible Say?

(A) Begin with worship.

As you will discover, the Book of Jeremiah is rich with symbolism, images, and metaphors. Perhaps one of the more familiar images is that of the potter (God) and the clay (us). This image is found in Jeremiah 18:1-6. A familiar hymn, "Have Thine Own Way, Lord," written by Adelaide Pollard, is based on this image found in Jeremiah.

The writer of this hymn was a religious activist in the early 1900's. She was feeling distressed in the midst of a fund raising campaign to secure money for a missionary trip to Africa. During this confused time she experienced a renewed relationship with God through her full trust in God's will for her. She expressed this renewed call by using the potter-clay image from Jeremiah (from *Companion to The United Methodist Hymnal*, by Carlton Young; Abingdon Press, 1993; page 38).

● Sing this hymn together as you open the session (*The United Methodist Hymnal*, 382).

(B) Answer the questions in the study book.

Remind participants that they can enhance their Bible study significantly by reading the biblical texts and answering the questions in their study books before the session.

● If they have already worked through the questions, spend ten to fifteen minutes sharing and discussing their answers.
● If class members have not yet worked through the questions in Dimension 1, allow them a few minutes to read them, along with the relevant biblical texts, either individually or in teams.
● Discussion of Dimension 1 questions might raise the following comments:

1. Jeremiah responds to Yahweh's words by protesting that he does not know how to speak, since he is only a boy. The Lord is not dissuaded by his objection, however, insisting that Jeremiah shall go where God sends him, speaking the words God commands him to speak. The Lord reassures Jeremiah, saying, "Do not be afraid of them, / for I am with you to deliver you" (1:8).

   Jeremiah's task is both destructive and constructive. God appoints him "over nations and over kingdoms" to "pluck up, to pull down, to destroy and to overthrow," but also "to build and to plant" (1:10). Only ten verses into this, the lengthiest of the Bible's prophetic collections, readers likely wonder about the meaning of these complimentary, yet also contradictory commands.

2. According to 1:16, the people of Judah are guilty of forsaking their own God, Yahweh, and of worshiping idols, the creations of human hands.

3. From the perspective of Jeremiah 2:7, Israel began to sin against Yahweh immediately upon leaving the desert and entering its God-given land.

   Jeremiah accuses God's people of forsaking "the fountain of living water" for cisterns, that is, pits dug from rock for water storage (2:13). God is a source of everflowing waters, yet Israel relies on underground vaults that cannot produce water, only store it. Moreover, Israel's cisterns leak and so are utterly useless! Behind Jeremiah's cistern metaphor lies the charge that Israel has abandoned its true God, only to rely on worthless idols.

4. Jeremiah 3:6-10 personifies Israel and Judah as sisters and Yahweh's wives in order to charge them with faithlessness. Both sisters have proved disloyal to Yahweh, their husband. Indeed, so wanton are they that their activity is likened to that of a prostitute (whose sexual activity recurs on a regular basis). Yahweh has divorced Israel on account of her unfaithfulness, as Judah knows. Yet she continues to engage in adulterous acts, that is, worshiping gods other than Yahweh.

(C) Consult the timeline.

● Examine the timeline in the study book (page 4) to help answer the following questions.
—Jeremiah 1:1-3 locates the prophet's ministry during the reigns of several Judean kings. What, according to the timeline in the study book, were the years of Jeremiah's ministry?
—What does the rapid succession of kings suggest about the stability of political affairs in Judah during Jeremiah's lifetime?
—When did Jeremiah receive God's call?
(According to Jeremiah 1:6, he was "only a boy.")
● Now ask class members these questions:
—How does the prophetic ministry of Jeremiah fit into the larger scheme of history?
—Note how Isaiah's and Jeremiah's prophetic ministries are related to the political situations of Israel and Judah.

(D) Investigate religious reforms.

● Share information from the "Additional Bible Helps" on "King Josiah's Reforms," found on page 37.
● Ask a gifted "orator" in your class to read 2 Kings 22:1–23:3. These verses describe how a scroll discovered in the Temple during the reign of King Josiah became the basis for covenant renewal and a series of important religious and political reforms.
● Remind class members that Jeremiah's early years of prophetic ministry coincided, at least in part, with Josiah's efforts at reform.
● Invite responses to the following questions:
—The reforms instituted on the basis of Deuteronomy 12–26 obviously enjoyed the full support of Judah's king. What other elements are necessary, however, if religious reforms are to succeed?
—Can you think of other historical religious reforms? What political situations surrounded these movements?

One answer to this question might be to note that the Protestant Reformation (Martin Luther as critical thinker and leader) and the rise of nationalism within Europe, which was then considered part of the Holy Roman Empire, both took place in the sixteenth century. This period of time marks the transition from the medieval feudalism to the centralized monarchies of the modern age.

(E) Focus on figurative language.

Jeremiah's poetry contains a rich array of metaphors and similes. These uses of figurative language invited Jeremiah's audiences to perceive issues and circumstances in particular ways.

● Divide class members into three groups; provide each group with newsprint, an easel, and markers.
● Ask group one to focus on Jeremiah 2:1-19; ask group two to focus on Jeremiah 2:20-37. Assign Jeremiah 3:1–4:4 to group three.
● Ask each group to identify Jeremiah's uses of figurative language in its assigned verses. How do these metaphors and similes function in Jeremiah's poetry?
● Responses to this assignment may include the following comments:

Group 1: Jeremiah 2:1-19.
—In 2:2, Israel's devotion to Yahweh during its post-Exodus wilderness trek is likened to the love of a bride for her husband. This metaphor emphasizes the intimate, exclusive nature of the relationship that

existed between Israel and Yahweh during Israel's early existence as a people.

—In 2:3, Israel is called the "first fruits of [the Lord's] harvest"—that is, the earliest and best of the produce, which belongs to God. Again, the metaphor functions to enhance our image of Israel during its early years.

—In 2:18, Yahweh accuses Israel of going to Egypt "to drink the waters of the Nile" and to Assyria "to drink the waters of the Euphrates." The drinking metaphor refers to the tendency of God's people to seek assistance and security from other nations, rather than from the Lord.

Group 2: Jeremiah 2:20-37.

—In 2:20, Jeremiah accuses Israel of "playing the whore." In other words, Israel, Yahweh's once-devoted wife (2:2), has become promiscuous, devoting herself to deities other than Yahweh. Here, the image of illicit, recurring sexual activity shapes our perception of Israel's idolatry, a profound betrayal of what should be a monogamous (faithful) relationship between Israel and its God.

—In 2:23-24, Israel is called a restive young camel (whose movement in any direction at any given time is totally unpredictable) and a wild ass in heat (whose determined search for a mate renders its stubborn movements utterly uncontrollable). Again, Jeremiah's choice of metaphors drives home Israel's senseless insistence upon rebelling against its God, while persistently pursuing other deities (the "Baals").

—In Jeremiah 2:26-27, the prophet mocks "the house of Israel" for engaging in pagan religious practices—here represented by those who say to a tree, "You are my father," and to a stone, "You gave me birth." Yet even those who engage in such foolish practices turn to Yahweh when times get tough (2:27). Are their entreaties in times of trouble sincere?

—Jeremiah 2:33 addresses Israel as a woman actively seeking multiple lovers. Again, wanton sexual activity functions negatively to characterize Israel's resort to other gods.

Group 3: Jeremiah 3:1–4:4.

—Yet again, an image of female sexual promiscuity shapes our perception of the people's idolatry (Jeremiah 3:1-3). Like a hardened prostitute, Israel refuses to be ashamed of "her" behavior.

—In 3:15, "shepherds" refers metaphorically to kings. Here, Israel is promised future, faithful rulers.

—In 3:22, the people of Israel are called "faithless children." The metaphor encourages thoughts of both headstrong youths and exasperated parents.

—In 4:3-4, both the breaking up of fallow ground and circumcising the heart refer to repentance.

● When each group has compiled its list of these and other metaphors, each should be permitted to share its findings with the class as a whole.

● Invite the entire class to reflect on the following questions:

—What do uses of figurative language contribute to our understanding of Jeremiah's oracles? Gather several responses.

—Is it surprising to you to read such explicit sexual language in the Bible?

—Why do you think that the prophet would have chosen such metaphors?

(F) Learn the story of Abiathar's expulsion from Jerusalem.

● Share the following background information with class members:

King David's son Adonijah (ad-uh-NIGH-juh) was next in line to the throne following the death of his older brother, Absalom. Though his bid for kingship had some support in high circles, David's younger son, Solomon, eventually succeeded his father as ruler of Israel.

Not long after David's death, Adonijah went to the queen mother, Bathsheba, with a request. He desired Abishag (AB-uh-shag), a member of the royal harem, as his wife. Bathsheba agreed to carry his request to Solomon, but her son interpreted Adonijah's petition as an indirect claim to the throne. Solomon ordered that Adonijah, his brother, be put to death.

Abiathar (uh-BIGH-uh-thahr), a priest serving in the Temple in Jerusalem, had been among Adonijah's supporters. In 1 Kings 2:26-27, King Solomon orders Abiathar's expulsion from Jerusalem. Henceforth, he shall live on his family estate at Anathoth (AN-uh-thoth). (You may want to read 1 Kings 2:26-27 aloud.)

Then tell class members this information: Jeremiah was likely a descendant of Abiathar (see Jeremiah 1:1), whose family had been removed from Temple service in Jerusalem. Some scholars suggest that in supporting King Josiah's religious reforms, with their insistence that the cult of Yahweh be centralized in the Jerusalem Temple, Jeremiah likely antagonized members of his own family, whose priestly prerogatives and practice in the region of Anathoth were threatened by the reform movement. Others propose, by contrast, that Jeremiah's family was involved in Josiah's reforming activities and became angry when he refused to support them fully. In any event, the prophet experienced intense conflict as a result of God's call on his life. Denied a wife and children of his own, he endured isolation and loneliness.

Old Testament prophets were people with personal histories and families. They suffered consequences from following God's call. Most of these prophets, as was Jeremiah, were embroiled in the political environment of their day.

- Ask for responses to the following questions:
  —How does our understanding of Old Testament prophets change when we realize the complex ways in which functioning as God's spokesperson affected their lives?
  —How does this model of faith in dialogue with political reality speak to us?
  —How does the separation of church and state impact this model of a politically active person of faith?

(G) Look for God in Jeremiah's poetry.

The God we encounter in Jeremiah's poetry is neither distant from nor immune to Israel's unfaithfulness. Neither can God be deceived by insincere words substituting for genuine repentance.

We should not assume that because Israel was unfaithful to its covenant obligations it did not participate in cultic practices designed to elicit Yahweh's help in times of trouble. In Jeremiah 3:2-5, we learn that the people, whose infidelity to God is described using the metaphor of female sexual promiscuity, nevertheless cry, "Father," when drought plagues the land.

- Ask a member of the class to read Jeremiah 3:2-5 aloud.
- After the reading, ask class members to share their thoughts about the God revealed in Jeremiah's poem.
  —What emotions does Jeremiah disclose?
  —What feelings would you experience if you were in God's position?
- Give class members the information in "Covenant Is a Two-Way Relationship," in "Additional Bible Helps," page 37.

Dimension 3: What Does the Bible Mean to Us?

(H) Find out how we are called by God.

In this learning option you will be inviting your class members to reflect on their own personal call by God.
- Read aloud the scriptural record of Jeremiah's call by God, Jeremiah 1:4-10.
- Discuss generally with class members Jeremiah's call.
  —When was he called?
  —What did God instruct him to do?
- Ask class members to divide into pairs and then share with their partner their experience of God's calling for them. Bear in mind that God does not call everyone to be prophets, but to be people of faith.
  Note that this may be difficult for some people. A way to begin to reflect on this would be to think about

the gifts and talents they have. How do they feel that these should be used? Have they ever felt these gifts affirmed by the church?

(I) Symbolize the emotions of God.

- For this learning option you will need construction paper of various colors, crayons, markers, and pencils. (You may want to bring glitter, glue, and other art supplies also.)
- Recruit three readers. Ask one person to read 3:19-20 and later 22a (God). Another reader will read 3:21 (a narrator type voice). The last voice will be Israel's children in 3:22b-24.
- Ask the readers to read the passage for the whole group.
- Then divide class members into groups of four. Ask the groups to create a symbolic representation of the passage. Emotions are high in this passage. We hear of God's disappointment and forgiveness.

(J) List Israel's sins and our sins.

- Divide class members into three or four groups. Provide each group with newsprint, an easel or stand, and a marker. You will need, as well, commentaries on the Book of Jeremiah.
- Ask each group to select a "scribe" who will record their responses to the following text.
- Suggest that another group member read aloud Jeremiah 2:26-28.
- Following the reading, ask groups to answer this question: What are Israel's sins, according to this passage?
- Answers likely will include the following:
  —Israel is like a thief, who regrets stealing only if caught.
  —Israel's leaders, including its religious leaders, are guilty of worshiping idols of wood and stone, rather than worshiping Israel's true God, to whom they owe absolute allegiance.
  —Yet in times of trouble, Israel cries out to Yahweh, as if its failure to be faithful to God was of no consequence. Clearly, the people expect God to be devoted to them, despite their refusal to honor their covenant obligations to the Lord.
- After identifying Israel's sins, ask groups to consider whether we share Israel's guilt:
  —Do we, like thieves, steal what is due the Lord, worshiping other "gods" instead: material possessions, social standing, our own self-importance?
  —Do we fail to cultivate a relationship with the Lord in all our daily dealings?
  —Do we turn to God only in times of distress, as if our relationship with God required no mutual, ongoing fidelity?
- At the end of fifteen minutes, invite each group to share several of its thoughts with the class as a whole.

(K) Sing a hymn of repentance for a closing worship time.

Charles Wesley's hymn, "Depth of Mercy," places on our lips the question, "Can there be mercy still reserved for me?" This query arises from the deep realization that we have failed to respond to God's claim on our lives. When we sing this hymn, we fervently ask God, "Now incline me to repent." Jeremiah, as we have seen, called on Israel to repent of its failure to honor its covenant with God.

● Join together in reading or singing this hymn of repentance (*The United Methodist Hymnal*, 355). Tell class members to look closely at the words as you sing.

Additional Bible Helps

King Josiah's Reforms

For over two centuries, the mighty Assyrian Empire held sway over much of Israel's ancient Near Eastern world. Eventually, however, it began to crumble; and with its decline, other nations—notably Egypt and Babylonia—jockeyed for power. Meanwhile, Assyria's vassal states, including Judah, nurtured hopes of restored territory and renewed national independence. During these uncertain yet exciting times, young Josiah became Judah's king.

According to 2 Kings 22, a crucial event occurred in the eighteenth year of Josiah's reign. In the midst of refurbishing the Jerusalem Temple, a scroll was discovered and brought to the king's attention. When Josiah heard the words of this scroll, he summoned a prophetess, Huldah, to confirm its authenticity. That scroll, biblical scholars agree, contained Chapters 12–26 of the Book of Deuteronomy.

Deuteronomy purports to be Moses' final address to the Israelites just prior to his death, as they prepared to enter the land of Canaan. The book undoubtedly contains some very old material. It is possible, however, that the scroll "discovered" in the Temple in 621 B.C. was a relatively recent compilation intended to buttress religious reforms based on a reinterpretation of Mosaic covenant faith for seventh-century Judah. Among its demands were absolute loyalty to Yahweh and the centralization of Israel's religious life.

Central to Mosaic faith as expressed in Deuteronomy was the concept of a "covenant" relationship between God and Israel. This deeply rooted tradition in Israelite religion asserted that God had entered into a conditional covenant with Israel at Mount Sinai. According to the terms of this conditional covenant, Yahweh—who chose Israel and brought it out of bondage in Egypt—promised richly to bless the people and to sustain and protect them in their God-given land. But God was not the only party to incur covenant obligations. Israel, for its part, was required to obey Yahweh's commandments and to love and worship God alone. The ultimate penalty for human disobedience was a rupture in the covenant relationship on which Israel depended for its very life.

Josiah threw his nation into religious reforms designed to bring it into compliance with the covenant demands set forth in Deuteronomy 12–26, including a regular service of covenant renewal. We should probably assume that during the early years of his prophetic ministry, Jeremiah supported Josiah's religious reforms, although the evidence is not so clear as we might like. Certainly the reform's emphasis upon Mosaic covenant faith would have appealed to the prophet, so long as the people's outward displays of piety were matched by sincere repentance and a genuine determination to comply with the covenant's requirements. Jeremiah did not lack for criticisms of his nation's doings; but at this stage in his prophetic ministry, he clearly believed that wholehearted repentance and obedience could elicit God's forgiveness of Israel's sins.

Covenant Is a Two-Way Relationship

We cannot understand Jeremiah's poetry unless we recognize how important the concept of covenant was to his ministry. When God offered a covenant relationship to Israel at Mount Sinai, the people freely accepted it, knowing what their covenant obligations would be. These obligations were not intended as a burden. Rather, they were designed to establish Israel as a nation of peace and justice, a holy people faithful to the holy God who had liberated them from slavery in Egypt, sustained them in the desert, and promised them a blessed existence in the land of Canaan.

The Old Testament nowhere considers the possibility that Yahweh might fail to honor God's covenant responsibilities. There is constant awareness, however, that human beings can fall short of the mark. Once Israel left the desert behind and began its new life in the land, it faced various temptations, including the temptation to rely less on its God and more on its own devices.

When troubles arose, of course, the people cried out to Yahweh. But Jeremiah charged that their resort to God was insincere; it grew out of pressing need, but would matter little once the problem passed. The people wanted a religion that "worked" for them, because it gave them everything they wanted and needed, but demanded little in return. Jeremiah reminded his audience that covenant relationship with the holy God is not something that was fixed in place centuries ago, making no demands upon those who enjoy its blessings today. To the contrary, relationship with God must be accepted by every individual within the communities of each generation if the people of God are to live abundantly, according to God's will.

8

Jeremiah 7:1-20; 26:1-19

*B*ETWEEN A ROCK AND A HIGH PLACE

LEARNING MENU

Bearing in mind the interests and needs of your class members, as well as those learning activities they enjoy best, select at least one learning segment from each of the three following Dimensions. Spend approximately one-third of your class time working on a Dimension 1 activity. Remember, however, that approximately two-thirds of class time should be spent on activities selected from Dimensions 2 and 3.

Dimension 1:
What Does the Bible Say?

(A) Open with a time of worship.

- Sing as a whole class the familiar African-American spiritual "There Is a Balm in Gilead" (*The United Methodist Hymnal*, 375). The chorus of this hymn was inspired by Jeremiah 8:22.
- If you have a pianist or guitarist (or other musician) among your class members, ask him or her ahead of time to accompany you in the singing of this hymn.

(B) Answer the questions in the study book.

- Remind class members that they can enhance their Bible study by reading and answering these questions prior to class time.

  If class members have already worked through the questions in Dimension 1, spend approximately fifteen minutes sharing and discussing their answers to the questions.

  If they have not worked through the questions before class time, provide a few minutes for reading the biblical texts and the questions, either individually or in teams.
- Discussion of the questions might evoke the following responses:
1. According to verses 5-6, God requires that the people of Judah practice justice in all their dealings, refrain from acts of violence (especially with powerless members of their society), and worship Yahweh alone.
2. According to verse 13, the people of Judah have persistently refused to repent of their sins, despite repeated divine overtures. Also note, in addition to the sins spelled out in verse 9 (recalling offenses prohibited in the Ten Commandments), the people are accused of placing confidence in the Temple (as a symbol of Yahweh's abiding, protective presence with Judah), despite their refusal to turn from their transgressions.

3. According to 7:20, God's consuming wrath will burn the land and all its life forms, including humans, animals, and vegetation.

4. An important feature of Chapter 26 is that a declaration of Jerusalem's fall had already been announced by Micah (Jeremiah 26:18). A very distinctive view of prophecy was developing. Prophecy could be very long delayed, but it would eventually take place. (For more information about this interrelatedness between Micah and Jeremiah read *Interpretation, Jeremiah*, by R. E. Clements; John Knox Press, 1988; pages 156–58.)

(C) Read parts in a play.

● Make photocopies of Jeremiah 26:1-19. Mark or highlight each person's lines.

● Assign the following roles and lines to persons in the class:
—Narrator: all verses and portions of verses that do not contain quotations by other characters;
—The Lord's words: verses 2-6, part of 18;
—Priests and prophets (excluding Jeremiah): parts of verses 8-9, 11;
—Jeremiah: verses 12-15;
—Officials and people: part of verse 16;
—Elders of the land: parts of verses 18-19.

● Give several minutes for the actors to look over their lines and to identify where they appear in the "play."

● Reenact the response to Jeremiah's Temple sermon by having people read their parts.

● After the reading, ask readers and the audience to discuss the drama.
—How serious is the threat against Jeremiah's life?
—Who are the "heroes" in the play?
—How does the quotation from the prophet Micah save Jeremiah's life?

● Finally, ask the narrator to read verses 20-24, the story of another prophet who spoke as Jeremiah had prophesied.

TEACHING TIP
Be prepared to help your readers with pronouncing the names in this passage:
Jehoiakim — ji-HOI-uh-kim
Josiah — joh-SIGH-uh
Judah — JOO-duh
Shiloh — SHIGH-loh
Micah of Moresheth — MIGH-kuh of MOR-uh-sheth
Hezekiah — hez-uh-KIGH-uh
Uriah — yoo-RIGH-uh
Shemaiah — shi-MAY-yuh
Kiriath-jearim — kihr-ee-ath-JEE-uh-rim
Elnathan — el-NAY-thuhn
Achbor — AK-bohr
Ahikam — uh-HIGH-kuhm
Shaphan — SHAY-fuhn

Dimension 2: What Does the Bible Mean?

(D) Investigate what happened to Shiloh.

Jeremiah's threat that the Lord will do to Jerusalem and its Temple what was done to the northern Israelite sanctuary at Shiloh (Jeremiah 7:12-15; 26:6) has little impact unless we know the story of Shiloh's downfall.

● You will need Bibles, Bible dictionaries, and commentaries on the biblical books of First Samuel and Psalms.

● Divide class members into two or four groups. Their assignment is to find out what happened to Shiloh.

● Ask half of the groups to read 1 Samuel 4—the account of the Philistines' capture of the ark of the covenant located at the Shiloh sanctuary—assisted by Bible dictionaries and commentaries.

● Ask the other half of the groups to read Psalm 78, especially verses 56-64, assisted by Bible dictionaries and commentaries.

● Ask the groups to read about the "Ark of Yahweh" (found in Bible dictionaries under "Ark" after the information on Noah's ark). A fuller understanding of the Ark of Yahweh will enrich this study on the events at Shiloh and the implications for Yahweh's followers.

● At the end of ten minutes, invite a representative from each group to report its findings to the class as a whole. Include in your discussion:
—What happened to Shiloh, and why?
—Why was this defeat so devastating?
—Report information about the Ark of Yahweh.
—In Psalm 78:58 a reference to "high places" is made. What does this mean?
—Where else have you read this reference? ("High places" refers to religious worship locations. Several "high places" are mentioned in the Old Testament. However, Jerusalem is the most sacred "high place.")

(E) Find out what the Lord demands.

The people Jeremiah addressed in stern tones with words of warning were on their way to the Temple to "worship the Lord" (Jeremiah 7:2). Obviously, their presence at the sacred site did not suffice to turn away the prophet's criticisms. Rather, Jeremiah challenged the lives they were leading outside the Temple gates.

Although Jeremiah delivered his Temple sermon over twenty-five hundred years ago, the divine demands he sets forth are timeless. (True, we do not make sacrifices to Baal or prepare cakes for the queen of heaven, but ours is a society that "worships" many things, including material possessions and financial security.)

- Read "Additional Bible Helps: Sickness of the Heart" (page 41) before using this learning option. The additional Bible information may prove helpful in leading the discussion.
- Ask a member of the class to read Jeremiah 7:21-26 aloud.
- Following the reading, ask people to identify Israel's overriding sin. What attitude motivates the people to steal, murder, and worship other deities?
  —Is this sin also a timeless problem for God's people?
  —What are our modern "idols"?
  —When are we most easily swayed in valuing our own accumulation of material objects over God?
  —When do we "walk in our own counsel, looking backward" rather than looking forward with our eyes on God?

(F) Debate two different types of covenant.

In Jeremiah 7 and 26, two different types of covenant collide:
  —The conditional Sinai covenant emphasizes human responsibility (persons and communities must honor their covenant obligations in order to remain in relationship with their holy God).
  —The unconditional Davidic covenant emphasizes God's initiative (the Lord promises to maintain a descendant of King David on the throne in Jerusalem forever).
- Divide class members into two groups. Ask each group to address the following questions:
  —What are the benefits of each type of covenant?
  —What potential problems does each type of covenant raise?
- Then ask one group to prepare to argue for the virtues of the Sinai covenant. Ask the other group to defend the virtues of the Davidic covenant.
- The groups may choose to work on their strategy together then decide on a spokesperson.
- Let the conversation begin!
- Allow about ten minutes (five minutes for each side) to hear the presentations.
- Where are Jeremiah's words in this debate? (Read in the study book "Outrage at the Temple," page 65.)

(G) Learn about Shaphan and his sons.

According to Jeremiah 26:24, Jeremiah was protected by Ahikam, son of Shaphan. Shaphan and his family were prominent in Jerusalem during Jeremiah's lifetime.
- For this activity you will need several Bibles, Bible dictionaries, and commentaries.

- Divide class members into groups of three or four persons each.
- Ask each group to learn what it can about Shaphan, his sons (Ahikam, Elasah, and Gemariah), and his grandson (Gedaliah).
- At the end of ten minutes, ask each group to report several of its findings to the class as a whole.
  —Since Jeremiah was protected by this family, what does this tell us about Jeremiah's "political connections"?
  —Was this a benefit or a detriment to Jeremiah's ministry? How so?

(H) Examine Jeremiah's eloquent defense.

In Chapter 2 of this study, we discovered that the ancient Israelites had difficulty distinguishing between true and false prophets. No single criterion for recognizing authentic prophets (fulfillment or nonfulfillment of a prophecy) could suffice in every situation.

As a result, prophets were handled with care. The death of the prophet Uriah, told in Jeremiah 26:20-23, is exceptional in this regard.
- Ask one member of the class to read Jeremiah's speech in Jeremiah 26:12-15 aloud.
- Ask class members the following question: By what argument does Jeremiah seek to save his own life in verses 14-15?

Dimension 3: What Does the Bible Mean to Us?

(I) Discover your symbols of security.

In his Temple sermon, Jeremiah charged that the people of Jerusalem trusted that the Temple's presence in their city would protect them from enemy assaults.

Jeremiah warned that unless the people were faithful to their covenant obligations, they, their Temple, their city, indeed their entire land would be destroyed.
- Divide class members into several groups. Ask each group to reflect on the following questions:
  —What are our "temples"?
  —In what religious symbols do we place our trust?
  —What gives meaning to these religious symbols?
  —Are these symbols intended to make a difference in how we live our lives beyond the walls of our church sanctuaries?
- At the end of ten minutes, invite a representative from each group to report its findings to the class as a whole.

(J) Find a prophet in your midst.

● Read "I Am a Prophet—True or False" in the "Additional Bible Helps" (page 42) before using this learning option. The article refers to ancient Hebrew prophets, but some of the characteristics would still hold true.

● For this learning option you will need paper, pens or pencils.

● Begin this learning option by saying:

"As you arrived at church today a woman was standing at the main entrance of your church building. She was calling out to all who passed by. A few church members stopped to talk to her. Others members hurried by with their hands over their children's ears. There was a lot of whispering about this woman at the beginning of church. Who was she? Where did she come from? Should the police be called? Was she crazy? But some of what she said was true."

● Divide class members into small working groups. Ask each group to write out a brief speech for this woman.

● After ten minutes invite a spokesperson from each group to read its speech.

● After these speeches, discuss these questions with the whole class:

—Are there prophets today? If so, who delivers these words from God? If not, how are God's words of judgment and direction communicated to people of faith?

—How receptive are we to God's words of justice and judgment?

—When and/or where have you heard "prophets"?

(K) Recite Psalm 24 for a closing worship time.

Psalm 24 contains three parts. Part one (verses 1-2) affirms the Lord's role as creator of all the earth. Part two (verses 3-6) asks who can approach the Lord's holy Temple in Jerusalem. The answer: only those living moral lives. Part three (verses 7-10) celebrates the return of the ark of the covenant, a symbol of God's glory, to the Temple, where it was kept in the Holy of Holies, the most sacred space within the Temple complex.

● Divide class members into two groups. Read through Psalm 24 responsively. Group One should read the odd-numbered verses; Group Two the even-numbered verses.

Note that this psalm, like others, *combines* an emphasis on the Jerusalem Temple as the dwelling-place of God's glory with moral mandates for those who would enter its precinct.

● Close with a prayer.

Additional Bible Helps

Sickness of the Heart

In the fourth edition of *Understanding the Old Testament* (Prentice-Hall, 1986; pages 399–400), Old Testament scholar and theologian Bernhard W. Anderson describes Jeremiah's diagnosis of the terrible "sickness" that plagued the people of his day:

Jeremiah agonized over the people's incurable sickness. They were, he said, a people with "a stubborn and rebellious heart" (Jer. 5:23). All Yahweh's discipline had failed. The word of the prophets had fallen on deaf ears; indeed, it had become an object of scorn to the people (6:10). With searching insight, anticipated by Hosea, Jeremiah perceived that the problem lay *within*—in the heart. To be sure, Israel's "sickness unto death" showed itself outwardly in many ways. The people were putting their trust in institutions: the Ark (3:16), the rite of circumcision (4:4), the Torah (8:8), sacrifice (7:21-26), the Temple itself (7:4). Moreover, the social bond of the covenant community was fractured. Every brother, said Jeremiah, was another deceitful Jacob (9:4-6). No one could be trusted, and oppression was heaped up like a pyramid. The people were like "well-fed stallions," each neighing for his neighbor's wife (5:8) and showing no concern for the defenseless victims of society (5:28). Blind nationalism, excited by the deceitful prophets, was rampant. And, idolatry was practiced not only in the Temple but on every high hill and under every green tree.

But these were only the outward symptoms of a problem rooted in the heart, the seat of human loyalties and devotion. Anticipating modern depth psychology, Jeremiah pointed out that the heart can cover up and justify ("rationalize") its real motives:

The heart is deceitful above all things,
and desperately corrupt;
who can understand it?
—Jeremiah 17:9 [RSV]

Yet there is no hiding place from the God who "probes the heart" in order to repay people with "the fruit of their deeds" (17:10). . . .

The catharsis—to use the language of psychology—had to come through crisis and catastrophe. . . . In the past, according to Jeremiah, Yahweh had shown forbearance. "Rising up early," to use the poetic expression for divine persistence, Yahweh had sent "his servants, the prophets." Moreover, Yahweh had tried the "shock treatment" of calamity with the purpose of bringing the people to their senses, but in vain. . . . At last Yahweh's patience was exhausted. "Weary of relenting" (15:6),

Yahweh had resolved to pour out divine wrath upon the people, destroying their idols and shaking the foundations of their existence.

As the prophet Jeremiah came clearly to see, the "catharsis" of "crisis and catastrophe" would come at the hands of Babylonian military forces.

I Am a Prophet—
True or False?

Determining whether a prophet was true or false was not an easy task. This task was officially left to the Temple priest. The following are some of the things he would take note of.

Characteristics of Hebrew prophets:
Hebrew prophets "emphasized the holiness of God, fearlessly criticized the morals of their own day, and taught a nobler way of living. They dealt with doomsday, with retribution, and with a return to the simpler, pious life. . . .

"The prophets did not separate [himself or herself] from the life of the people. . . .

"The prophets were intensely patriotic and scornful of all who would invade their land" (*Harper's Bible Dictionary*, by Madeleine S. Miller and J. Lane Miller; Harper & Brothers, 1952; page 582).

False prophets could be mercenary—"more interested in their salaries than in true prophetic utterance. False prophets had no inspired message; were motivated by self-interest; and preferred popularity to a truly helpful ministry. . . . False prophets as well as true ones could have visions" (*Harper's Bible Dictionary*; pages 584–85). Women were not excluded from this false prophecy profession.

For more detailed information use *Harper's Bible Dictionary*. This resource has several pages on prophets and many Scripture references. A more recent edition of *Harper's Bible Dictionary* (by Paul J. Achtemeier; 1985) is also available. The entry for *prophet* in this edition would be a good resource also.

9

**Jeremiah
11:18–12:6;
15:10-21;
17:14-18;
18:18-23;
20:7-13, 14-18**

"THE LORD IS WITH ME LIKE A DREAD WARRIOR"

LEARNING MENU

Based on your knowledge of class members—their interests, needs, and preferred learning styles—select at least one activity from each of the three following Dimensions. Spend approximately one-third of your class time working on a Dimension 1 activity. Approximately two-thirds of your time should be spent on activities selected from Dimensions 2 and 3.

Dimension 1:
What Does the Bible Say?

(A) Open with a time for worship.

● Begin your class time with a few moments of silence. Then offer a prayer of guidance for today's time together. The prayer could be something like:

All Knowing God,
You are the one who called the great prophets of old to take your word to a sin-filled world.
You are the one who continued to love your people even though their actions were turning them farther away from you.

Help us today to hear again with new ears your prophetic words.
Help us to hear our own call to be your servants in today's world.
Amen.

(B) Answer the questions in the study book.

● Remind class members that they can enrich their Bible study by reading the lesson and reflecting on these questions before class time.
● If class members have already worked through the questions in Dimension 1, spend fifteen minutes sharing and discussing responses.
● If they have not worked through the questions ahead of time, allow them a few minutes to read through the biblical texts, along with the questions, either individually or in teams.
● Discussion of Dimension 1 questions might bring out the following issues and answers:
1. Jeremiah wishes to see God's retribution on his enemies. That is, he asks Yahweh to judge and punish them in proportion to their sins against the prophet.
2. God's interrogative proverbs constitute a challenge to Jeremiah. If he cannot race with foot-runners, what chance has he with horses? If he cannot survive in "safe

land," how can he hope to negotiate difficult terrain? These questions function both as challenge and as warning. From God's perspective, Jeremiah should steel himself for tougher times ahead.

3. Jeremiah's opponents mock him because his predictive prophecies have not yet been fulfilled. Jeremiah knows that he has served Yahweh, faithfully proclaiming God's authentic words. He asks God to shame his foes, not him! "Let them be dismayed, do not let me be dismayed," he cries. Divine justice demands that they be punished, so far as Jeremiah is concerned. But he requests that they be destroyed with "double destruction"!

4. Jeremiah curses both the day of his birth and the person who brought to his father the news that a baby boy had been born. He does not, however, curse God or his parents.

(C) Paraphrase Jeremiah's laments.

● Divide class members into six groups (or three groups taking two laments each). Assign one of Jeremiah's personal laments to each group: Jeremiah 11:18–12:6; 15:10-21; 17:14-18; 18:18-23; 20:7-13; 20:14-18.
● Ask each group to compose a short paraphrase of the contents of its lament.
● These questions may help the groups focus their paraphrases:
  —What concerns is Jeremiah bringing to God?
  —What cultural or historical situation does Jeremiah find himself in?
  —What response does Jeremiah want from God?
● At the end of ten minutes, ask a representative from each group to share its paraphrase, in whole or in part, with the class as a whole.

Dimension 2: What Does the Bible Mean?

(D) Take a closer look at costs of the prophetic calling.

● For this learning option you will need to have paper, crayons, markers, magazines, newspapers, scissors, and glue.
● Divide class members into four groups. Direct them to the art supplies.
● First, ask a member of each group to read Jeremiah 15:16-18 aloud.
● Then discuss these questions:
  —What does verse 16 affirm? (Jeremiah has served as God's mouthpiece.)

—What image is in verse 17?
—Yahweh's "hand" rests heavy upon him. What is Jeremiah's charge against God (verse 18)? Where is Yahweh's support? (Rather than sustaining him in his endeavors, the prophet complains, Yahweh has not "cured his wounds." In fact, Jeremiah feels that God has proven an unreliable source of healing and strength. "Truly, you are to me like a deceitful brook, like waters that fail" [verse 18]. *Wadis* dried up quickly, and so were unreliable sources of water. Jeremiah's wadi metaphor asserts that God, too, is untrustworthy.)
—How will the Lord respond to such a charge?
● After the groups have delved into the Scripture passage, challenge them to take these images and make a pictorial representation of these verses. They may draw or use words or pictures cut from newspaper. Do not limit creativity!
● After ten to fifteen minutes ask each group to show their work to the whole class.
● Then you may choose to enter into a full class discussion about the costs of prophetic calling. Jeremiah was faithful. Yet sometimes he questioned God's support. What is our "cost" for being servants of God? Does God offer us support? If so, how?

(E) Analyze Jeremiah's rhetoric.

Rhetoric may be defined as the art of persuasion. Speakers and writers often use various rhetorical techniques in order to persuade their audiences toward certain perceptions, judgments, and beliefs. Jeremiah was a master orator.

In his laments, Jeremiah enlisted a number of rhetorical techniques in his attempt to elicit responses from God.

In 11:20, for example, the prophet addresses Yahweh as "you, O LORD of hosts, who judge righteously, / who try the heart and the mind." He then goes on to request that the Lord bring retribution against his foes. In this context, "O LORD of hosts" emphasizes God's power, while reference to Yahweh's righteous judging of heart and mind supports the judgment against those who plot against Jeremiah's life. The final line of verse 20, "for to you I have committed my cause," reminds God of Jeremiah's utter dependence on the One he serves and of God's obligation to sustain him.

● Divide class members into two groups. Share the above information with them. Assign one of the following passages to each group: Jeremiah 18:20-23; 20:7-11.
● Ask each group to analyze the functions of rhetorical techniques in its passage.
  —Does Jeremiah use rhetorical questions? similes? metaphors?

—How do his choices of language advance or detract from the points he wishes to make?
- At the end of ten minutes, ask a spokesperson for each group to lead a discussion of that group's text. Members of each group should feel free to participate in this discussion.

(F) Explore Jeremiah's concept of God.

The contents of Jeremiah's laments reveal a great deal about who he believes God is and how he believes God acts. (Of course, his thoughts about these topics may have been quite different when he was severely depressed, as opposed to when he was not.)
- Divide class members into six groups or three groups, assigning one or two laments to each group (Jeremiah 11:18–12:6; 15:10-21; 17:14-18; 18:18-23; 20:7-13; 20:14-18).
- Ask group members to discuss what their lament or laments reveal of Jeremiah's thoughts about God.
- After ten minutes, let each group present its findings to the class.
- Ask class members to reflect on their own thoughts about God during times of distress and/or depression. If members of the class are willing to share their reflections with the whole class, invite them to do so.
- Alternatively, replace the last step with this one: ask class members to divide into pairs. Ask them to tell each other remembered thoughts and feelings they had about God during difficult times.

(G) Make a collage.

- For this activity you will need magazines (including news magazines), scissors, markers, and glue.
- Before class time read in "Additional Bible Helps," "Breaking Through Denial," page 47. You may want to share some of this information with class members during this learning option.
- Divide class members into groups of three to four people.
- Ask each group to construct, by using the words and images of Jeremiah's laments (Jeremiah 11:18–12:6; 15:10-21; 17:14-18; 18:18-23; 20:7-13; 20:14-18), a collage that shows visually either Jeremiah's state of mind or, in cases where Yahweh responds, God's state of mind.
- At the end of fifteen minutes, invite each group to share its collage with the class as a whole. Groups may display their collages in the classroom for the remainder of their study of Jeremiah.

(H) List your expectations of religious leaders.

- For this activity you will need newsprint or large sheets of paper, an easel, and a marker or a chalkboard and chalk.
- Tell class members: "All of us have certain expectations of our religious leaders. Some of those expectations are shaped by personal experience. Others are molded by social stereotypes.

  "Think about religious leaders you know—clergy, religious educators, hospital chaplains, Sunday school teachers. Perhaps you know members of religious orders in the Roman Catholic Church. You may be friends with a local rabbi.

  "Even if you do not know many such persons, you undoubtedly hold certain expectations of them."
- List on the chalkboard or on large sheets of paper your expectations of religious leaders.
  —How does the Jeremiah revealed in his personal laments stand in relation to those expectations?
  —Have any of your expectations of such leaders changed in light of your reading and reflection upon Jeremiah's complaints?

(I) Think about human relationships.

- Present the information in the following paragraphs to class members:

  Jeremiah found at least some support in the upper ranks of Judean society (read 26:16). In his personal laments, however, Jeremiah describes himself as surrounded by opponents, in whose ranks could be found family members, (once-)close friends, fellow prophets and other religious leaders, and so on. Moreover, the Book of Jeremiah asserts that the Lord forbade the prophet to marry and have a family of his own.

  In his complaints, Jeremiah appears to be in dialogue only with God. Many of us might affirm, however, that our relationship with God frequently is mediated through the love, concern, support, and even the constructive criticism of those persons closest to us.
- Ask class members now to imagine how Jeremiah's experiences might have been different had he enjoyed the fellowship and support of immediate family. Discuss the following questions:
  —Could such relationships have strengthened Jeremiah's ministry? If so, how?
  —Or was it necessary for Jeremiah to stand essentially alone? What benefit is there to be unencumbered by close human relationships?

—Think of your own life and its responsibilities. How have you chosen to live it—alone or among supportive family and friends? Discuss the balance you have achieved between a faithful life within the church and with your friends and family.

(J) Write a lament.

Jeremiah's laments reflect the prophet's thorough knowledge of Israel's religious traditions. In the aftermath of Jerusalem's destruction, these prayers were used to express the Judeans' own feelings of frustration, despair, and hope in God. They have continued to serve that function down through the centuries. "Whenever we are struck by misfortune," Nobel Laureate Elie Wiesel writes, "we turn to [Jeremiah] and follow in his footsteps; we use his words to describe our struggles" (*Five Biblical Portraits*; University of Notre Dame Press, 1981; page 101).

● Provide each class member with paper and a pencil or pen.
● Remind them of features common to ancient Israelite laments:
 —an initial address to Yahweh;
 —expressions of confidence in God;
 —details of one's complaints (the words of opponents, God's neglect);
 —pleas for vindication;
 —words of praise.
● Encourage class members to compose their own, brief laments. If persons in the group are uncomfortable doing so, another option would be to ask them to write a lament that might properly be placed in the mouth of a person or persons suffering in the midst of a contemporary world crisis (a refugee; a homeless person; someone suffering from flood, earthquake, fire).
● At the end of ten minutes, ask volunteers to share their laments with the class as a whole *or* simply with another member of the group.

(K) Identify contemporary "Jeremiahs."

● Ask class members to think for a few moments about persons they know, people in newspaper headlines, and characters in books, plays, and films who in some way remind them of the Jeremiah we encounter in his personal laments.
 —What qualities does Jeremiah share with such persons and characters?
 —Are such persons and characters heroes, villains, or some combination of both? Are they effective leaders, or simply disrupters of the status quo? Explain your answer.
 —Would you welcome such persons and characters into

your church congregation? your workplace? your home? Why, or why not?

(L) Close the session with prayer.

● Invite your class members to unite in prayer on behalf of modern-day counterparts to the characters in the Book of Jeremiah.
 —Pray for persons who survive only by denying certain realities in their lives.
 —Pray for those who suffer the hatred and ridicule of others.
 —Pray for our religious leaders, who sometimes struggle with feelings of loneliness, of unrealistic expectations placed upon them, of divine abandonment.
 —Pray for God's sustaining power as we take up our tasks of servanthood.

Additional Bible Helps

Jeremiah's Voice Can Be Ours
The pages of Hebrew Scripture are filled with intriguing characters, and their stories have captured the imaginations of generations of Jews and Christians. It comes as something of a surprise, therefore, to realize that the biblical writers' interest in sharing these characters and stories was not really biographical. When details of a prophet's life appear in a book bearing his name (such as Hosea's marriage), we can be sure that those details were integrally related to that prophet's oracles.

Jeremiah's complaints—deeply personal as they may strike us—were not preserved simply as witnesses to one person's suffering. Later generations of Jews found in his laments expressions of thoughts and feelings with which they, too, struggled. Consider for a moment Jeremiah's cries for vindication against his foes. In the aftermath of Jerusalem's destruction, survivors undoubtedly questioned why they should endure so much, while enemy nations serving other gods murdered their families and helped themselves to their land and possessions. Under such circumstances, they added their voices to Jeremiah's pleas that God destroy his enemies in proportion to the destruction they had wrought. When they felt abandoned by their God, they echoed the prophet's desire for Yahweh's sustaining power, comfort, and deep healing.

Indeed, the oracles of all Israel's prophets were preserved in large measure because subsequent generations discerned in earlier oracles God's words for their own day. The Word of God was neither perishable nor disposable—devoid of meaning once its original historical context had passed. To the contrary, that Word spoke afresh in ever-changing contexts. When we study the Bible's prophetic literature and reflect on sermons based on its verses, we continue the ever-enlivening process of reinterpretation.

Breaking Through Denial

From the beginning of his prophetic ministry, Jeremiah attempted to catch his audience's attention, to convict them of their sinfulness, to convince them of the necessity of true repentance and return to Yahweh their God. As years passed and the people persisted in the behaviors and attitudes Jeremiah condemned, the prophet's words became increasingly harsh, as did the responses of his adversaries. Jeremiah faced opposition at every turn—from family members, fellow Judeans, religious leaders, other prophets, and members of the royal court.

On the one hand, Jeremiah could expect no less. His oracles were filled with terror, divine wrath, and criticism upon criticism. Surely he knew that his audiences would respond with defensiveness, denial, and hostility. On the other hand, Jeremiah was a man, not a puppet. His proclamations did not pertain to a people far removed from his own life, experiences, and emotions. When he foretold Judah's destruction, he was talking about the end of his own people and nation. The sins that both tore and enraged God's heart wreaked havoc within Jeremiah's own as well. When his audiences spurned God's words, Jeremiah also felt the sting of rejection.

10

Jeremiah 24;28–29

BABYLONIA: THE FOE FROM THE NORTH

Dimension 1: What Does the Bible Say?

(A) Open with worship.

In today's lesson you will be discussing "the foe from the north." War, refugees, dislocation—are all important elements in today's lesson.

- Read aloud Psalm 137. This psalm contains strong emotions—the emotions present during this time of crisis for Israel and Judea.

(B) Answer the questions in the study book.

- Discussion of Dimension 1 questions might move in these directions:

1. According to Jeremiah 24:5-7, the basket of good figs represented the exiles deported to Babylon in 597 B.C. The basket of spoiled figs (24:8-9) represented the Judeans remaining in Palestine and those in Egypt.

2. Hananiah first asserts that Yahweh has "broken the yoke of the king of Babylon," that Babylonian control of the region will end. He then prophesies that Yahweh will return to the Temple the precious vessels taken away in 597 B.C. He further proclaims that the Lord will return to Judah King Jeconiah (jek-uh-NIGH-uh) and all the exiles deported to Babylonia. Obviously, the loss of the Temple vessels weighed heavily on the Judeans, who perceived in their loss an affront to Yahweh.

3. Without benefit of body language, vocal inflection, facial expressions, it is difficult to know whether Jeremiah's initial response, "Amen! May the LORD do so; may the LORD fulfill the words that you have prophesied," was sincere, or was intended to mock Hananiah. Jeremiah's next words drew upon prophetic precedent. Past prophets were known to have uttered prophecies of doom. The optimistic words of any prophet should be evaluated with caution and accepted only when his or her predictions had been fulfilled.

Hananiah responded by physically removing from Jeremiah's neck a yoke—signifying Babylonia's power over the region—and breaking it. "Thus says the LORD," he said, "This is how I will break the yoke of King Nebuchadnezzar [neb-uh-kuhd-NEZ-uhr] of Babylon from the neck of all the nations within two years."

4. The Lord was instructing them to settle into life in Babylonia, building houses, planting gardens, marrying, and giving their children in marriage. Moreover, the exiles should pray for the city of Babylon's welfare, since their fate was linked to its own. Further, God instructed the exiles not to allow themselves to be deceived by the prophets and diviners in their midst, since God was not speaking through them.

(C) Learn about the Babylonian Empire.

- For this activity you will need Bible dictionaries and Bible atlases, paper, pencils or pens, newsprint and a stand, and markers, or a chalkboard and chalk.
- Divide class members into groups of three or four.

Part One:

- Ask each group to use the Bible dictionaries and atlases to learn as much as it can about the Babylonian Empire.

Part Two:

- Tell groups also to look for the following information on how the exiled Judeans lived in Babylon:
  —What were some of the new professions the Judeans learned in Babylon? (farming, weaving, dyeing, metal-working, banking)
  —Did some Judeans obtain wealth while in captivity? If so, how? (married women from wealthy families)
  —What financial system was adopted? (coined money)
  —What religious worship and education system was developed during exile? (the synagogue)
  —What encouraged the writing down of the Pentateuch and other Old Testament books that became the Hebrew Bible? (absence of well-loved sacred scenes and time to ponder God's will for the nation)
- At the end of the time, ask one member of the class to record all the groups' findings.

Dimension 2: What Does the Bible Mean?

(D) Consider the fig.

To add a little something extra to today's lesson, you may want to bring a box of figs to share with class members.

So small a thing as a reference to figs in Jeremiah 24 can shed light on life in ancient Israel. Literal and figurative references to figs and fig trees appear over sixty times in our Bible, testifying to their importance in biblical times.

- You will need Bibles, Bible dictionaries, concordances, paper, and pencils or pens for this activity.
- Divide class members into groups of three or four members each.
- Ask members of each group to read about figs in a Bible dictionary. Encourage them, further, to look up biblical passages containing both figurative and literal references to fig trees and their fruit.
- At the end of ten minutes, invite a representative from each group to report to the whole class the results of each group's research.
- At the end of the learning option pass around a basket of figs—fresh or dried will be fine.

(E) Imagine the impact of Jeremiah's letter.

- Divide class members into units of four to six persons. Ask each person to assume a family role within the unit (mother, father, elderly in-law, teenager, young child).
- Ask one member of each unit to read aloud Jeremiah's letter, 29:4-14. Then, ask each "family member" to reflect on its significance for him or her. Will the reactions of wide-eyed teenagers be the same as their grandparents' responses?
- At the end of ten minutes, invite each "family" to report its responses to the whole class.

(F) Examine prophetic conflict.

- In order to set the scene for this activity, present the following points to class members:
  Both Old Testament stories about prophets and collections of prophetic oracles (such as the Book of Jeremiah) strongly suggest that prophetic activity increased during turbulent times.
  Prophets competed with one another for the attention and support of their audiences. Jeremiah was forced to contend with prophets, both in Judah and in Babylonia, whose oracles directly contradicted his own.
  Like his adversaries, Jeremiah sought to discredit contrary voices. In Jeremiah 23:13-15, for example, he roundly criticized both the past prophets of Samaria, capital of the defunct Northern Kingdom of Israel, and the prophets of Jerusalem.
- Read Jeremiah 23:13-15 aloud, noting that Jeremiah goes so far as to compare these prophets to the inhabitants of Sodom and Gomorrah.
  In the face of such charges and countercharges, the people of Judah likely felt uneasy and confused. Who should they believe?

- Divide class members into three or four discussion groups.
- Ask half the participants of each group to identify reasons why Hananiah's prophecies might seem credible. (Recall what was said in a previous lesson about Davidic/Zion theology [study book, pages 63–66].) Ask the other half of each group to identify reasons why Jeremiah's prophecies might seem credible. (Recall what was said in a previous lesson about Sinai covenant theology [study book, pages 66–67].)
- At the end of ten minutes, ask representatives from each group to tell the high points of their discussion to the rest of the class.

(G) Discover the power of symbols.

- For this learning option you will need large sheets of paper and markers or chalkboard and chalk. Also draw a large picture of an animal's yoke to show to class members.

- Our Judeo-Christian tradition is rich with symbols. Ask class members to name some religious symbols. Write these on the large sheets of paper or on the chalkboard.
  —Are any of the symbols listed considered both religious and political?
- It is doubtful that *yoke* will be mentioned by any class member as a religious symbol. However, this wooden frame used to join two draft animals for pulling or field work was a symbol of political and religious subjection for Jeremiah.
- After giving the above information to class members, ask someone to read Jeremiah 28:1-11.
- Then divide class members into small groups.
- Ask them to discuss the following:
  —Talk about the image of Jeremiah walking around with a wooden cattle yoke upon his shoulders.

—Show class members the illustration in the first column on this page.
—Diagram or write out the prophetic debate between Jeremiah and Hananiah.
—How did Hananiah use the symbol of the yoke to gain support for his false prophecy?
—When have you seen religious symbols used to support nonreligious events or thoughts? (One example is Ku Klux Klan cross burnings.)
- End with a general discussion on the importance and impact of the use of religious symbols.

Dimension 3:
What Does the Bible Mean to Us?

(H) Roleplay the words "behind" your conversation.

How often we find ourselves speaking words that disguise, rather than reveal, our true thoughts and feelings! At the workplace we exchange pleasantries with a coworker who is openly critical of our performance around other employees. We graciously accept invitations to social occasions from persons whose time we would rather not share.

Such compromises are part and parcel of everyday life. They preserve our socially acceptable selves. They enable us to get along with coworkers, friends, the couple running the local market—even family members at times. They are important to the quality of our lives.

Problems arise, however, when the words we speak become routine, empty, devoid of genuine content.
- Ask four class members to be part of a roleplaying exercise. Give your volunteers a few minutes to select a topic they would like to discuss. Ask them to stand facing each other in normal, conversational poses. As each person makes a contribution to the conversation about work conditions, politics, and so on, however, ask that person to turn toward the rest of the class and say aloud what he or she *really* thinks and feels about what's been said.
- After the roleplay, invite class members to reflect on the words they routinely say in regular worship settings (such as the Lord's Prayer and the Apostles' Creed). To what extent do they "mouth words"?
  —Do their words connect with how they really think and feel? Why, or why not?
  —What, if any, implications do these words have for life outside the sanctuary?
- Ask persons in the class to share their reflections if they wish to do so.

Jeremiah charged that his fellow Judeans mouthed empty words of contrition and repentance in troubling times, but revealed their true selves in how they acted.

(I) Evaluate a contemporary catastrophe.

- In preparation for this learning option, read in the "Additional Bible Helps" the section on Theodicy, page 52.
- For this activity you will need a chalkboard and chalk or a marker, newsprint, an easel or other stand, or a large piece of paper. Ask one class member to act as the group's "scribe."
- Drawing from national news reports and newspaper headlines, select a story concerning human suffering, either within the United States or elsewhere in the world (the conflict in Bosnia, drug addiction, AIDS, and so on).
- Ask class members to discuss the following questions:
  —How, given his cultural presuppositions and theological premises, might Jeremiah have spoken to such a calamity?
  —How might he describe God's relationship to human suffering in that particular situation?
  —In what ways might our understandings and approaches to the current crisis differ from Jeremiah's, given our own presuppositions and theological beliefs?
  —In what ways do we, as Christians, understand God's relationship to persons and nations undergoing such catastrophes?

(J) Sing for strength in tribulation.

Charles Albert Tindley's hymn, "Stand By Me," speaks of God's sustaining presence *with* those who are in tribulation.

- You will need several hymnals for class members to use ("Stand By Me" appears on page 512 of *The United Methodist Hymnal*). If hymnals are not available, copy the words of the hymn on a piece of newsprint posted where all can see.
- Ask a musical member of the class to lead the others in singing all five stanzas of the hymn.
- When you have finished singing, lead class members in a prayer on behalf of those in our world who are suffering.

Additional Bible Helps

Jeremiah Proclaims God's Punishment.
Throughout the Book of Jeremiah, repeated assertions link Judah's demise to the people's sin. Yahweh is merciful, but even divine mercy cannot forever hold back God's punishment upon a relentlessly corrupt, rebellious people. To be sure, Jeremiah's God is capable of grief, as well as wrath, when considering Judah's offense:

O that my head were a spring of water,
    and my eyes a fountain of tears,
so that I might weep day and night
    for the slain of my poor people!
O that I had in the desert
    a traveler's lodging place,
that I might leave my people
    and go away from them!
For they are all adulterers,
    a band of traitors.
They bend their tongues like bows;
    they have grown strong in the land for
        falsehood, and not for truth;
for they proceed from evil to evil,
    and they do not know me, says the LORD.
                    (Jeremiah 9:1-3)

In these verses, it is impossible to distinguish Jeremiah's tears from the Lord's own. Nevertheless, in many of the book's passages, Jeremiah's God appears in the role of judge and ultimate executioner.

So negative a perspective inevitably placed Jeremiah in opposition to many groups. As we have seen, his own family opposed him, at least at times during his prophetic career. He alienated, indeed, enraged a number of Jerusalem officials. None of these conflicts exceeded, however, Jeremiah's contentious relationship with Jerusalem's religious leaders, its priests and prophets. Time and time again, he included these two groups in charges and denunciations:

The priests did not say, "Where is the LORD?"
    Those who handle the law did not know me;
the rulers transgressed against me;
    the prophets prophesied by Baal,
    and went after things that do not profit.
                    (Jeremiah 2:8)

The prophets prophesy falsely,
    and the priests rule as the prophets direct;
my people love to have it so,
    but what will you do when the end comes?
                    (Jeremiah 5:31)

For from the least to the greatest of them,
    everyone is greedy for unjust gain;
and from prophet to priest,
    everyone deals falsely.
They have treated the wound of my people
        carelessly,
    saying, "Peace, peace,"
    when there is no peace.
                    (Jeremiah 6:13-14)

As these and other texts make clear, Jeremiah had little respect for those religious leaders whose true motivations, in his opinion, included personal profit from those Judeans hungry for words of reassurance.

Frequently, Jeremiah accuses other prophets of lying. Because distinguishing between true and false prophets and their prophecies was always problematic, and Jeremiah's prophetic opponents could base their messages on beliefs associated with Davidic/Zion theology, Jeremiah's conflicts with other intermediaries, including Hananiah, were often rancorous. After Jerusalem was destroyed, however, and his prophecies were realized, did Jeremiah finally command the respectful attention of those not exiled to Babylonia? As we shall see in the following lesson, even the fulfillment of his dire predictions failed to convince Jeremiah's fellow Judeans that they should assent to his words.

THEODICY: THE QUESTION OF GOD'S JUSTICE

Many biblical passages claim (or assume) that God rewards the righteous and punishes those who do evil. But human experience suggests otherwise; in real life it often seems to the careful observer that the innocent do suffer, while the evil prosper.

The problem we encounter when we believe in a God of justice and yet see that injustices continue to happen on earth is sometimes called "theodicy" (thee-OD-uh-see). This term comes from the Greek words for God (*theos*) and justice (*dika*).

Theodicy asks the question: If God is all-powerful and all-good, why does God allow innocent people to suffer? People have tried to resolve this theological and logical dilemma in a variety of ways. Naturally, evil does not fit nicely into one theological category. But hopefully the following views will be helpful in continuing to address theodicy in our modern world.

A *theodicy of protest* questions God's goodness, asking why an all-powerful God would allow the slaughter of children, the Holocaust, and other atrocities. If God were good, God would answer prayers of help, which seem to be ignored.

Process theodicy maintains that God is good but questions the nature of God's power, claiming that God's power is persuasive rather than absolute and that there is evil that is outside of God's control. God simply does not have the power to prevent all tragedies and suffering. Nevertheless, God is a constant influence for ultimate good.

Free-will theodicy claims that because God gave humans the freedom to choose between right and wrong, our suffering is a result of our own choices for evil. This theodicy fails to account for "natural" evil such as floods, earthquakes, famine, and disease.

An *educative theodicy* claims that suffering is ultimately good because it provides an opportunity for growth. Suffering deepens character, strengthens com-passion, and nurtures creativity, as well as increases our appreciation for good. However, people do not necessarily have to suffer in order to achieve these characteristics, and this theodicy ignores the fact that many people are completely destroyed by their suffering. Ultimate human growth cannot be justified easily by the waste of life.

An *eschatological theodicy* claims that if people experience compensation after death for evil suffered in life, then their suffering is not in vain. The promise of a just reward received in an after-life (end-time, or eschaton [ES-kuh-tahn]) is a comfort to many who suffer, but it is often used as an excuse for failure to remedy unjust situations in this life and subjugates people to lifetimes of oppression. Placing all hope in a future of bliss negates the possibility of living life to the fullest in the present.

A *theodicy of mystery* emphasizes the inability of human beings to understand God's purposes. Many times, Christians are taught to trust in a theodicy of the mystery of God's goodness and mercy, having blind faith that God's purpose will triumph over evil. While this is a popular theodicy, it diminishes the capacity for human relationship with God.

In a *theodicy of communion*, Christians have identified the suffering of Jesus as God's own suffering with humanity. Through willing suffering for others, humans have the opportunity for a deeper intimacy with God. However, even the redemptive quality of suffering for others (based on the suffering servant of Isaiah 53 and Jesus as Messiah) can be misused if it glorifies suffering and invites victims to remain passive in the face of evil.

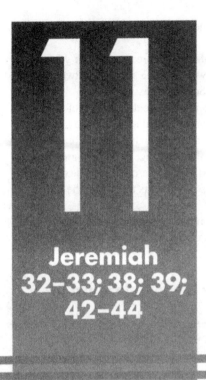

11

Jeremiah 32–33; 38; 39; 42–44

TALES FROM PRISON TO EGYPT

LEARNING MENU

Keeping in mind the interests and needs of your class members, as well as those learning activities they most enjoy, select at least one option from each of the three following Dimensions. Dimension 1 focuses readers on the biblical texts—the first and most crucial step! Spend approximately one-third of your session working on a Dimension 1 activity. Remember, however, that approximately two-thirds of class time should be spent on activities selected from Dimensions 2 and 3.

Dimension 1:
What Does the Bible Say?

(A) Open the session with a worship time.

● Ask class members to form a prayer circle.
● Invite one class member to lead the group in prayer on behalf of political prisoners around the globe.
(Depending upon how interests run in your class, you may want to contact Amnesty International, 404-876-5661, to learn specific information about political pris-

oners around the world and about how church groups can be involved in this ministry.)
● Ask another class member to pray for those who put themselves—their time, their possessions, perhaps even their lives—on the line for others.
● Close the prayer with thanks to God for hope and healing in times of trouble.

(B) Answer the questions in the study book.

● Remind class members that they can enhance their Bible study significantly by reading the biblical texts and answering the questions in their study books prior to class time.
● If they have already worked through the questions, spend ten to fifteen minutes sharing and discussing their answers.
● If class members have not yet worked through the questions in Dimension 1, allow them a few minutes to read them, along with the relevant biblical texts, either individually or in teams.
● Discussion of Dimension 1 questions might raise the following comments:
1. Because Jeremiah perceives the Lord's involvement in the matter, he agrees to buy the property in Anathoth and carefully carries out the detailed legal procedures.

Entrusting the deed to Baruch, he proclaims God's oracle that "houses and fields and vineyards shall again be bought in this land." But afterward he prays to Yahweh; and his words, "Ah Lord GOD!" suggest Jeremiah's doubts about the transaction.

2. Jeremiah is removed from the cistern by Ebed-melech the Ethiopian, who intercedes with King Zedekiah on the prophet's behalf. Ebed-melech does not stop with words. He then gathers the men, the ropes, and the cushioning rags that will insure Jeremiah's safe and painless rescue.

3. Yahweh's response begins with a conditional promise. If the people remain in their homeland, Yahweh will "build you up and not pull you down; . . . plant you, and not pluck you up." Indeed, God goes so far as to say "I am sorry for the disaster that I have brought upon you"—an extraordinary admission (verse 10). The people need not fear the king of Babylonia, for the Lord will save, rescue, and have mercy on them. But if the people refuse to stay in their land and flee to Egypt, then, God threatens, they will die by sword, famine, and pestilence. This is the familiar triad that functions so often in the Book of Jeremiah and elsewhere to express God's punishment upon sinful people. In essence, then, God's words present the petitioners with a clear and crucial choice. Having promised faithfully to follow Yahweh's directive through Jeremiah, the people are told in no uncertain terms what will be the penalty for disobedience.

4. Jeremiah's audience in Egypt boldly informs him that they will not listen to "the word that you have spoken to us in the name of the LORD" (44:16). After all, Jeremiah's prophecies concerning Jerusalem's fate were confirmed by historical events. The fulfillment of a prophetic word was widely regarded as evidence of a prophet's accuracy (see Deuteronomy 18:22 for a negative statement of this criterion). Yet both men and women insist that they shall continue to serve "the queen of heaven," a prominent goddess in Israel's ancient Near Eastern world. Notice that in verses 25-30, Jeremiah sarcastically says, "By all means, keep your vows and make your libations!" But he then pronounces God's intention to punish them for their sins.

Dimension 2: What Does the Bible Mean?

(C) Investigate the right/obligation of land redemption.

- For this activity you will need several Bibles; commentaries on Leviticus, Jeremiah, and the Book of Ruth, or several one-volume commentaries; paper, and pencils or pens.

- Divide class members into three groups. (If your class is large you may want to have six groups, two groups working on each Scripture passage.)

- Ask each group to investigate the concept of land redemption. Relevant biblical texts include Leviticus 25:25-28; Ruth 4; and Jeremiah 32:6-15. Reading the commentaries on these passages will help group members understand what is going on in these texts.

- Assign one of these three texts to each of the three groups.

- At the end of ten minutes, invite a representative from each group to share its findings with the class as a whole.

(D) Illustrate the joyful return to Judah.

- Attach strips of newsprint to one wall of your classroom until you have a surface three feet wide and five to six feet long.

- You will need markers, crayons, magazines (including news magazines), construction paper of bright vivid colors, party hats, streamers, scissors, and glue.

- Ask a member of the class to read aloud Jeremiah 33:10-11.

- Ask each person to use the art supplies you have gathered and his or her creativity to contribute to a mural showing joyful scenes that will be part of restored life in Judah.

- Class members may choose to wear party hats while creating the mural or may choose to incorporate them into the mural.

- Display the mural in your classroom.

(E) "Reason" with Jeremiah.

Throughout his prophetic ministry, Jeremiah functioned as a "peripheral" prophet. That is, he subjected the status quo to a radical critique and sought, through words and deeds, to overturn it—even if doing so brought enormous human suffering.

When Jeremiah urged the besieged inhabitants of Jerusalem to desert to the Babylonians, his words sounded like pure sedition. Jerusalem's leadership—including its priests and prophets—reacted with disgust and anger, mingled perhaps with fear (Jeremiah 38).

- Ask a gifted orator in the class to read aloud the gripping narrative in Jeremiah 38:1-28. Ask another class member to assume the role of Jeremiah, and ask four other participants to play the parts of his opponents.

- Imagine Jeremiah's accusers confronting the prophet with their charges. What other arguments might they have given to support their view that Jeremiah's proclamations of doom were ill-timed and inappropriate?

- "Jeremiah" should, in turn, respond to their arguments out of his own understanding of the Lord's role in Jerusalem's imminent destruction.
- Members of the "audience" should feel free to prompt the players with arguments of their own.
- At the end of ten minutes, ask the roleplayers and other class members to respond to the dispute.

(F) Interview Ebed-melech for the "News at Six."

- Recruit someone to read aloud Jeremiah 38:1-13 and 39:15-17.
- Ask one class member to play the role of Ebed-melech. Ask another member to assume the role of a television interviewer. Don't forget the film crew! Give your volunteers a few minutes to "get into character."
- As film rolls for the 6:00 P.M. news broadcast, the interviewer should question Ebed-melech about his role in the daring rescue of Jeremiah from the muddy cistern.
  —How did Jeremiah's plight come to his attention?
  —Was the prospect of approaching King Zedekiah daunting?
  —What was Jeremiah's response to his rescuers?
  —Is Ebed-melech concerned about the reactions of Jeremiah's opponents?
  —Is he expecting some reward for his efforts?
- After the interview discuss with the whole class the encounter. Were there ways they would have responded differently? Did hearing and seeing people act out this scene add a new dimension to the understanding of the event? If so, how?

TEACHING TIP
Pronunciation Guide
Shephatiah — shef-uh-TIGH-uh
Mattan — MAT-uhn
Gedaliah — ged-uh-LIGH-uh
Pashhur — PASH-huhr
Jucal — JOO-kuhl
Shelemiah — shel-uh-MIGH-uh
Malchiah — mal-KIGH-uh
Chaldeans — kal-DEE-uhnz
Zedekiah — zed-uh-KIGH-uh
Ebed-melech — ee-bid-MEE-lik

(G) Study a map.

- You will need a Bible dictionary for this activity.
- Locate the geographical settings for events told in Jeremiah 41:11–44:30. Look at the maps on page 62 and on the inside back cover of this book.

- Read 41:1-10 to get some background information on Ishmael. Then discuss these questions with your class:
  —Where were Gedaliah and the Babylonian garrison stationed? (41:1)
  —To what location did Ishmael son of Nethaniah flee with his eight men? (41:15)
  —At what places in Egypt did Jewish communities settle? (43:7; 44:1)
  Yahweh's vehement rejection of Egypt as a settling place for those Judeans not exiled to Babylonia stirs memories of Israel's earlier exodus from that land. Ammon, too, was an ancient and enduring foe of Israel.
- Ask a class member to check a Bible dictionary (under *Ammon* or *Ammonites*) for information concerning the enmity between Ammon and Israel and to report his or her findings to the class.
- Discuss how references to these two nations affect the narrative impact of Jeremiah 42–44.

(H) Write an account of Gedaliah's assassination for your local newspaper.

- For this activity you will need to have paper and pencils or pens.
- Prepare ahead of time a synopsis of Jeremiah 42–44. Read your synopsis to class members before starting this activity.
- Ask class members to compose a newspaper article on the breaking story of Gedaliah's assassination. They may wish to work in groups or individually.
- Remember the who, what, where, and why of journalism. Make use of "anonymous sources" and "government insiders."
- At the end of ten minutes, invite class members or groups to read their articles to the entire class.

(I) Roleplay Jeremiah's conflict with his fellow Judeans in Egypt.

- Ask members of the class to assume the roles of Jeremiah and the men and women in his audience (Jeremiah 44).
- Allow time for the characters to read Chapter 44 prior to their roleplay.
- After a few minutes of preparation time, ask the cast of characters to reenact the biblical scene. They need not slavishly follow the biblical speeches, but should feel free to improvise.
- After the roleplay (and a round of applause), ask the whole class to reflect on the different perspectives motivating the responses of both Jeremiah and his audience.

(J) Learn about the "queen of heaven."

- For this activity you will need several Bibles, Bible dictionaries, and commentaries on the Book of Jeremiah; pieces of paper and pencils or pens.
- Divide class members into groups of three or four members each.
- Ask the groups to learn what they can about the "queen of heaven." Be sure to follow-up on Scripture passages cited in the dictionary, as well as cross-listings.
- At the conclusion of ten minutes, ask each group to share two of its findings with the class as a whole.

Dimension 3:
What Does the Bible Mean to Us?

(K) Find God's revelation in this text.

A biblical scholar has suggested that we begin to discern the significance of a biblical text when we ask the question, "Where is God's revelation in this text?" At the end of this lesson in the study book, we considered this question in relation to Jeremiah's purchase of his cousin's plot at Anathoth. There, it was suggested, God's revelation comes in the form of the Lord's question, "is anything too hard for me?"—a question that points to the Lord's absolute power and freedom to interject unexpected hope into even the most desperate of circumstances.

- Divide class members into three groups:
  - **Group One**—Jeremiah 33
  - **Group Two**—Jeremiah 38
  - **Group Three**—Jeremiah 44
- Ask each group to answer the question, "Where is God's revelation in this text?"
- At the end of ten minutes, ask a spokesperson from each group to share its findings with the class as a whole.

(L) Share stories related to Jeremiah's experiences.

- For this learning option you will need crayons, markers, pencils, and construction paper of various colors.
- Encourage class members to think about a time of personal crisis when words and/or actions brought unexpected glimmers of hope.
- After a few minutes of reflection, pass around a basket of art supplies. Encourage everyone to draw a symbol of a time in their life when words or actions brought unexpected glimmers of hope.
- After several minutes ask for volunteers to tell their stories and show their symbols to the whole class.
- Ask class members to recall a time when someone they

know—personally or through the press—has taken a daring risk to help a person or persons in danger. Again, request that volunteers share their stories with the entire group.
   —How are these events similar to events in Jeremiah's life?
   —Tell what symbols of hope you found in Jeremiah's experiences.

(M) Write a hymn of thanksgiving.

- For this learning option you will need paper and pencils or pens.
- Ask several class members to take turns reading aloud Jeremiah 33.

   In this chapter we once again hear and perhaps even sense God's great love for creation. God truly wants to be in relationship with humanity.

- Divide class members into working pairs. Give them paper and pencils or pens. Explain that each pair will write a line or phrase of thanksgiving. Ask them to write something that their congregation is thankful for. Begin each phrase with "Give thanks to the Lord of hosts."
- After the pairs have worked a few minutes, begin your hymn of thanksgiving. Ask each pair to contribute to the hymn.
- Begin with:
   "Give thanks to the Lord of hosts,
      for the Lord is good,
      for his steadfast love endures forever!
   Give thanks to the Lord of host, . . ."
- Now add the lines and/or phrases from the pairs.
- Conclude by repeating the beginning sentence.
- This hymn of thanksgiving could be incorporated into a Sunday morning worship time. Talk with your pastor about this possibility.

(N) Read responsively.

Psalm 22 appears in the Psalter of *The United Methodist Hymnal* at No. 752. If class members enjoy singing, try singing Response 2. Have someone who is comfortable leading singing teach this sung response and sing it where you find the large red "R."

- You will need sufficient copies of the hymnal, or of Bibles of the same translation, for every two class members.
- Read the Psalm responsively. Ask one member of the group to read the light type and the rest of the class members the dark type. Or ask the men to read the light type and the women the dark. Or ask one half of the class to read the light type and the other half the dark type. Be creative in how you assign the reading.
- After the reading, ask class members to think of words in the Psalm that remind them of Jeremiah's feelings

and experiences. At what points do their own lives intersect with the psalmist's prayer?

- Allow a few minutes for responses. Then, close the session with prayer. A suggested prayer might be:
    Gracious God,
        To whom we have trusted,
        To whom we have sought for deliverance.
        Give us strength to hear your words of comfort
            and hope.
        Direct us in ways of servanthood.
        Help us to feel in our hearts your care.
    Amen.

Additional Bible Helps

A Look at Authorship

In previous lessons, we have most frequently read Jeremiah's words in the form of poetic oracles. A quick survey of other biblical books reveals that most of Israel's prophets prophesied primarily, though not exclusively, in verse. (In many Bible translations, oracles judged to be poetry are arranged in verse on the printed page, while prose materials run continuously from the left margin to the right.)

In the chapters we have examined for this lesson, prose narrative predominates. (Though poetry is present, as well; note, for example, the brief hymn of thanksgiving in Jeremiah 33:11b, the taunt song in 38:22, and the poetic oracle in 43:11.) In some cases, these narratives are cast in first person speech—that is, Jeremiah tells what is happening (as in Jeremiah 32). In others, Jeremiah is referred to in the third person (or does not appear in the narrative at all), and the narrator is anonymous. Frequently the prophet is shown as giving speeches and lengthy prayers.

Who is responsible for these narratives and for their presence in the Book of Jeremiah? Many scholars believe that Baruch played an important role in writing the narratives extending from 36:1 through 45:5. On the one hand, Chapter 36 begins with an account of how Baruch recorded from dictation God's oracles through Jeremiah, writing them in a scroll. On the other hand, Chapter 45 concludes with God's word to Baruch. The scribe is weary and finds no rest (45:3). But God promises him, "I will give you your life as a prize of war in every place to which you may go" (verse 5).

But the Book of Jeremiah did not attain its final, canonical form during the lifetime of the prophet or his scribe. Later editors contributed to the shaping of the Jeremiah tradition as well. These editors clearly were influenced by the theology set forth in the Book of Deuteronomy and that continues in the telling of Israel's history contained in the books of Joshua, Judges, Samuel, and Kings (the so-called Deuteronomistic History). Yet the latest layers of the Book of Jeremiah reflect the future hopes of even later editors, who returned to the prophet's words again and again for inspiration in the shaping of their own hopes for Israel.

12

*T*HE IRRATIONAL PERSISTENCE OF HOPE

Jeremiah 30–31

LEARNING MENU

Keeping in mind the interests and needs of your class, as well as those learning activities they most enjoy, select at least one learning segment from each of the three following Dimensions. Dimension 1 focuses upon the biblical texts themselves—the first and most crucial step! Spend approximately one-third of your session working on a Dimension 1 activity. Remember, however, that approximately two-thirds of class time should be spent on Dimensions 2 and 3.

Dimension 1:
What Does the Bible Say?

(A) Open with a time of worship.

- This is the concluding lesson on the Book of Jeremiah. You may want to begin by reading aloud some of the verses that have been especially meaningful to class members.
- A responsive reading that goes well with the lesson is found in *The United Methodist Hymnal*, page 741. This Psalter reading is based on Psalm 4 with the sung response from "There is a Balm in Gilead" (Jeremiah 8:22).

- You will need enough hymnals for class members to share. This familiar refrain can be sung a cappella (without music). As you read responsively, try singing the response at the large red "R."

(B) Answer the questions in the study book.

- Remind participants that they can enhance their Bible study significantly by reading the biblical texts and answering Dimension 1 questions prior to class.
- If they have already worked through the questions, spend ten to fifteen minutes sharing and discussing their answers. If class members have not yet worked through the questions in Dimension 1, allow them a few minutes to read them, along with the relevant biblical texts, either individually or in teams.
- Discussion of Dimension 1 questions might raise the following comments:
1. Jeremiah 30:6 invites readers to perceive the anguish and terror evoked by "that day" (the Day of the Lord) through the symbolic lens of a woman experiencing the anguish of childbirth. Ancient Israel did not downplay the agonies accompanying even the normal delivery of children. In Israel's ancient Near Eastern world, however, giving birth was a hazardous undertaking, since complications could endanger the lives

of both mother and child. Many other biblical texts draw on travailing woman metaphors and similes to express physical and psychological agony. In some texts, the assertion that men will act like women in labor appears in curses. (Often our modern literary critics favor new metaphors over recurring ones.) Biblical poets show no preference for new metaphors; rather, they frequently drew from such stock phrases, entrusting their messages to traditional imagery.

2. According to Jeremiah 30:10, God will save the exiles, bring their children out of captivity, and secure them in their own land.

3. Yahweh promises that what Israel's enemies have done shall be done to them. The devourers will be devoured, the captors will go into captivity, the plunderers will be plundered, those who prey will be preyed upon.

4. The proverb about sour grapes says that children suffer the consequences of their parents' actions.

5. According to Jeremiah 31:33-34, Israel will no longer need to be taught Yahweh's Torah ("instruction") because God will place it within them, inscribing it on their hearts.

(C) Choose and carry a text.

- Insure that every class member has access to a Bible, paper, and a pencil or pen.
- Ask each participant to read Jeremiah 30–31, either alone or in pairs.
- Then ask them to identify fewer than five verses that they would like to write down and carry in their wallets or keep in their Bibles for the next year. Encourage everyone to write these verses on the paper provided.
- When all have written their selected verses, invite them to share their passages with at least one other person, explaining why they chose those particular texts.
- Then everyone should fold his or her paper and place it in a wallet or Bible.

Dimension 2: What Does the Bible Mean?

(D) Explore the concept of the "Day of the Lord."

- For this activity you will need Bibles; Bible dictionaries; commentaries on Amos, Isaiah, and Zephaniah; paper; and pencils or pens.
- Divide class members into several small groups.
- As noted in the study book page 97, the "Day of the Lord" was originally associated with that time when

Yahweh would destroy Israel's enemies. A number of Israel's prophets, however, proclaimed that the "Day of the Lord" would be a time of judgment upon Israel for its sins. After Judah's demise in 587 B.C., references to the "Day of the Lord" again referred to the future age when God would destroy hostile nations.

- Review study book information and the above information on "Day of the Lord" with class members.
- Then assign each group a passage or two from the following list:
   Amos 5:18-20
   Isaiah 2:10-22
   Isaiah 13:6-13 (against Babylon)
   Isaiah 34:8-15 (against Edom)
   Zephaniah 1:7-18
- Ask each group to study its assigned biblical passage or passages, using the dictionaries and commentaries available.
- Some questions your small groups may want to address are these:
   —How do these accounts of the "Day of the Lord" compare with the Jeremiah accounts in today's lesson?
   —Are metaphors or similes used? If so, what are they?
   —What feelings do these accounts of the "Day of the Lord" convey?
   —Do any of these passages contain familiar Scriptures?
- At the end of ten minutes, ask a representative of each group to share several of its findings with the class as a whole.

(E) Compare homecoming texts from two prophetic traditions.

- You will need newsprint or a large sheet of paper and a marker for each group.
- Ask a good reader to read aloud Jeremiah 31:7-14.
- After the reading, divide class members into three or four groups. Then assign one or more of the following texts from the Book of Isaiah to each group:
   Isaiah 35
   Isaiah 40:9-11
   Isaiah 41:17-20
   Isaiah 43:19-21
   Isaiah 49:8-12
- Ask each group to compare Jeremiah 31:7-14 with its Isaiah text or texts. Someone in each group needs to list both similarities and differences between the texts on the sheet of paper.
- At the end of ten minutes, ask each group to report the results of its work to the class as a whole.

(F) Read the story of Rachel.

The story of Rachel, wife of Jacob and mother of Joseph and Benjamin, is told in Genesis 29:9–35:24. Daughter of Laban and sister of Leah (who also was married to Jacob), Rachel died giving birth to her second son. Rachel appears also in the New Testament (Matthew 2:18), in a quotation from Jeremiah 31:15.

● You will need several Bibles, Bible dictionaries, commentaries on Genesis and Matthew, paper, and pencils or pens for this activity.

● Divide class members into groups of three or four.

● Ask each group to learn what it can about Rachel's life and death. (Articles on "Rachel" in Bible dictionaries will summarize her story for you, if time does not permit reading through the chapters in Genesis.)
   —How does knowing about Rachel's life inform your readings of Jeremiah 31:15 and Matthew 2:18?
   —Can you think of other biblical examples where stories are woven throughout the Bible?

● At the end of ten minutes, invite a representative of each group to report its findings to the class as a whole.

(G) Explore biblical female images of God.

● Before class time read in the "Additional Bible Helps" found in this chapter the article on "Female Images for God." Also read the article found on page 68, "Female City Imagery in Hebrew Poetry." Be prepared to share this information with class members.

● Ask class members to read and discuss the following biblical passages containing female images of God. They may be surprised to discover that such texts are included in our Hebrew Scriptures!

● Divide class members into four discussion groups. Assign each group one of the following passages:

Group One:
—In Isaiah 42:14-17, Yahweh takes up the travailing woman simile to describe God's own behavior. Conventionally an image of human responses to terrifying events, the simile here functions to describe the effects of Yahweh's gasps and pants.

Group Two:
—In Psalm 90:2, childbirth imagery functions to illumine Yahweh's creation of the earth:
   "Before the mountains were born,
   before the earth and the world came to birth,
   you were God from all eternity and for ever."
                                   (*The Jerusalem Bible*)

Group Three:
—In Deuteronomy 32:18, childbirth imagery describes God's creation of Israel:
   "The Rock that begot you, you neglected,
      you forgot the God
         who labored in anguish with you."
                            (writer's translation)

Group Four:
—In Isaiah 66:13, Yahweh promises to comfort Jerusalem's inhabitants "as a mother comforts her child."

● Your small groups may also want to look at the passage in today's lesson that has female imagery—Jeremiah 31:18.

● The following questions may help begin the small group discussion:
   —Why do you think these early prophets and writers used female images in reference to God?
   —What do these images communicate to you? (Do answers generally differ between the men and women in your class?)
   —Why do you think that these female images of God have often been overlooked when Scriptures are chosen for worship?

Dimension 3: What Does the Bible Mean to Us?

(H) Imagine new images of God.

The people of ancient Israel developed metaphors for God that made sense within their own cultural context—for example, God as father, as mother, as powerful manifestations of nature, as a warrior more powerful than the mighty empires of the day and their deities, as protective shepherd.

● For this learning option you will need large sheets of paper and markers or chalkboard and chalk.

● Ask class members to reflect aloud about metaphors for God that are meaningful within their own cultural, communal, and personal contexts.

● As class members share these metaphors, record them on the sheets of paper or on the chalkboard. You may want to denote repeated answers, not to "vote" for the most popular, but only to note which metaphors are most often used. Be sensitive that some people have very strong investments in how they personally address God. The hope of this learning option is to show the variety of ways God has been addressed.

● This imaginative exercise can provide group members with meaningful new metaphors that can enrich their prayer lives.

- Close with some general observations about the metaphors recorded. (That these images of God are just avenues through which we try to understand the complexity of the Holy One. Any one image thought to be the only way to think of God actually limits God.)

(I) Compose a prayer.

- Divide class members into three or four groups. Make sure every one or two participants has a copy of the study book.
- Allow five to ten minutes for groups to look back over the lessons on Jeremiah, identifying those themes, topics, and ideas that bear special significance for contemporary life.
- Ask each group to compose a prayer rooted in the Jeremiah traditions.
- At the end of five to ten minutes, ask a representative from each group to lead the class in its prayer.

(J) Join in singing "Amazing Grace."

- Provide class members with the words to "Amazing Grace" (*The United Methodist Hymnal*, 378).
- Stand and sing this great hymn, remembering God's promises and everlasting love.

Additional Bible Helps

The Renewed Covenant

In Jeremiah's day, Davidic/Zion theology was prominent. According to that theological perspective, Yahweh entered into an eternal covenant with David and his descendants, promising that one of David's line would always sit on the throne in Jerusalem. As years passed the belief arose that God would never allow Jerusalem, with its Solomonic temple, to be destroyed.

Jeremiah's oracles announced yet another covenant relationship between God and Israel. According to the covenant forged at Sinai, following Israel's exodus from Egypt, both God and Israel incurred responsibilities. Yahweh promised to give Israel a homeland, to bless and protect the nation throughout generations. Israel, for its part, was obligated to keep God's Torah—those instructions, laws, and teachings by which the people might live faithfully in relationship with Yahweh and with each other. According to Jeremiah, Israel had failed so miserably to keep God's Torah that finally, the ancient covenant was broken.

In oracles of hope and restoration, however, the Jeremiah tradition speaks of a renewal of the covenant relationship between God and Israel. As we have seen, the covenant formula, "you shall be my people, and I

will be your God," is reasserted in Jeremiah 30:22.

Given Israel's track record of sin and rebelliousness, what could insure that history would not repeat itself? In Jeremiah 31:31-34, Yahweh speaks of a "new covenant" with Israel, one that cannot be severed because the people will "know" their God in the most pervasive and profound way. God will place the Torah within them, inscribing it upon their hearts. Their knowledge of God's teachings will no longer depend on human willingness or memory. At Yahweh's initiative, the future of the once-conditional covenant will be secured:

But this is the covenant that I will make with the house of Israel after those days, says the LORD: I will put my law within them, and I will write it on their hearts; and I will be their God, and they shall be my people. No longer shall they teach one another, or say to each other, "Know the LORD," for they shall all know me, from the least of them to the greatest, says the LORD; for I will forgive their iniquity, and remember their sin no more.

(Jeremiah 31:33-34)

In the Book of Ezekiel, a text reminiscent of Jeremiah 31:31-34 also promises that a divinely wrought change within the hearts of the Babylonian exiles will insure the perpetuation of their covenant with Yahweh:

I will give them one heart, and put a new spirit within them; I will remove the heart of stone from their flesh and give them a heart of flesh, so that they may follow my statutes and keep my ordinances and obey them. Then they shall be my people, and I will be their God.

(Ezekiel 11:19-20)

Female Images for God

Indeed I heard Ephraim pleading:
"You disciplined me, and I took the discipline;
    I was like a calf untrained.
Bring me back, let me come back,
    for you are the LORD my God.

(Jeremiah 31:18)

Is Ephraim my dear son?
    Is he the child I delight in?
As often as I speak against him,
    I still remember him.
Therefore I am deeply moved for him;
    I will surely have mercy on him,
        says the LORD.

(Jeremiah 31:20)

The "I" who speaks in verse 18 and is addressed by Ephraim (=Israel), her dear son, is not Rachel, but Mother Yahweh. (A number of female metaphors for Yahweh appear in the Hebrew Scriptures; until recently they have been largely overlooked.) Ephraim confesses his past rebelliousness, the disgrace of his youth, but also begs to be allowed to return (verse 18). And "Mother" Yahweh responds out of her deep yearning for him. Commentator Robert P. Carroll writes, "Every time she speaks of him she remembers just what he means to her and her insides moan for him. . . . So she most surely will have mercy on him. . . . Yahweh's love for Ephraim is so strong, so visceral, that the child will encounter mercy in spite of his foolish youthfulness" (*Jeremiah: The Old Testament Library*; Westminster, 1986; page 600).

In verses 31:21-22, another shift in metaphor appears: suddenly, Israel is addressed as a young woman, a faithless daughter wavering in her decision to come home. She is urged to set up road markers for herself, to return to her cities. Verse 22b is one of the most puzzling lines in all of Hebrew Scripture. The meaning of the phrase, "a woman encompasses a man," has resisted the efforts of countless interpreters. At most we can say that the new thing Yahweh has created on the earth indicates a reconciliation. Is Jerusalem the "woman," and does her protective encircling of a man envision the presence of Yahweh, her Warrior King, in her midst once more? (See Zephaniah 3:14-20.)

13 CRY ALOUD TO THE LORD!

Lamentations 1–5

Dimension 1:
What Does the Bible Say?

(A) Open with a time of worship.

- As mentioned in the study book on page 111, "Morning Has Broken," *The United Methodist Hymnal*, 145, is based on Lamentations 3:22-23. This would be an appropriate hymn with which to begin today's session.

- Another option would be to use "An Order for Morning Praise and Prayer," found in *The United Methodist Hymnal*, 876.

(B) Answer the questions in the study book.

- Remind class members that they can enhance their Bible study significantly by reading the biblical texts and answering the questions in their study books prior to class time.
- If they have already worked through the questions, spend ten to fifteen minutes sharing and discussing their answers.
- If class members have not yet worked through the questions in Dimension 1, allow them a few minutes to read them, along with the relevant biblical texts, either individually or in teams.
- Discussion of Dimension 1 questions might raise the following comments:
1. In Hebrew, the common word for "city," `ir, is a feminine noun. Hebrew poets often personified cities as women. When the author of Lamentations personified

Zion as a maiden, he invited his audience to perceive the city as beautiful, tender, delicate, and vulnerable. Suddenly, however, the vulnerable woman has become a mother bereaved of her children, a helpless female without protectors and afflicted by physical abuse. Personifying Jerusalem as "Maiden Zion" or "Daughter Zion" both permits the lamenters to express the intensity of their pain over her suffering and invites God to pity this unprotected, defenseless, solitary woman.

2. Without exception, these verses assert God's responsibility for Jerusalem's plight. God has acted in anger, showing no mercy. On account of God's rage, Jerusalem was left defenseless before her enemy. The Lord assumed the role of an enemy warrior, bending the bow and killing Zion's inhabitants. Yahweh has destroyed the king's palace and burned the Temple built hundreds of years earlier during Solomon's reign. God has breached Jerusalem's walls. Note that nothing is said of the Babylonian army—they are merely the instruments of God's wrath.

3. According to Lamentations 2:14, Judah's prophets failed to pronounce its iniquity and to move the people to repentance. In order to please their audiences, these establishment prophets proclaimed soothing oracles of their own creation. Israel's prophetic literature bears witness to the people's unwillingness to take seriously those prophets who criticized their actions and called them to repentance and life in obedience to the Lord. Too late the people realized that the prophets of doom spoke truth, while the peace-speaking prophets deceived them.

4. These laments are more than acute expressions of grief. They are addressed to Yahweh, and they intend to effect a response in Judah's God. Images of women cannibalizing their children in order to survive, of priests and prophets lying dead within the sanctuary, and of corpses on every street corner seek to catch God's attention and to arouse God's divine pity and mercy.

(C) Experience an ancient Israelite lament.

- Ask class members to sit quietly, their feet on the floor, arms relaxed, and eyes closed.
- Tell them to visualize the images and to experience the emotions conveyed in Lamentations 1:1-22 as you read the text aloud in a slow, solemn voice.
- When you have finished reading, give class members several minutes to reflect silently on what they have seen with their mind's eye. After three minutes, ask them slowly to open their eyes.
- Allow ten minutes for class discussion of what they have experienced.

—What images came to mind during this reflection time?
—What feelings did you experience?
—Did any phrase or image especially speak to you?

(D) Visualize Jerusalem's plight.

- For this activity you will need several news magazines, posterboard, scissors, and glue.
  The tragedy endured by Jerusalem's inhabitants becomes real to us when we show it using pictures from contemporary trouble spots around the world.
- Divide class members into groups of three persons each.
- Ask a member of each group to read Lamentations 4 aloud.
- Then ask each group to make a collage, using the art supplies you have gathered, that illustrates the catastrophes described in Lamentations 4.
- Be sure to include the biblical lamenter or lamenters in your collage.
- You may also want to include conversation "bubbles" for the lamenters on the collage.
- After fifteen minutes, ask each group to show its artwork to the whole class.

Dimension 2: What Does the Bible Mean?

(E) Learn more about biblical laments and dirges.

- For this activity you will need several dictionaries, Bible dictionaries, Bibles, paper, and pencils or pens.
  Historically laments have played an important role in Jewish and Christian traditions. However in our contemporary culture, piety tells us to suppress our deep feelings of loss and pain. Our ancient brothers and sisters of faith were very honest with God regarding their feelings. In this learning option you will be looking more closely at these ancient laments.
- Divide class members into groups of three or four.
- Ask them to study the meaning of *lament* and *dirge*. Look up the words in a dictionary (Webster's or other English language dictionary).
  —How do these two words differ by definition?
  —Think of brief cultural examples for each of these words. (An example may be given in the dictionary.)
- Now look at biblical laments:
  —Ask one person in each group to look for examples in the Book of Lamentations.
  —Ask another person in each group to look for exam-

ples in the Book of Psalms. (Some examples are: Psalms 13; 22; and 88.)

—Ask another person to look for examples in the Book of Job.

- Each group may want to address these questions:
  —What generally do laments have in common?
  —Did you find any examples of laments that could also be dirges?
  —Can you think of a contemporary example of a religious lament or dirge?
- At the end of ten minutes, invite a representative from each group to share what it has learned.

(F) Assume the roles of the lamenters and Lady Zion.

- Divide class members into groups of four.
- Ask three group members to read aloud the words of the lamenters in Lamentations 1:8, 9a, 10-11a, and 17. Ask the fourth group member to read aloud the words of Maiden Zion in Lamentations 1:9b, 11b-16, and 18-22. Encourage them to read their verses with appropriate emotion.
- After a few minutes, ask group members to share their feelings about the words they have read.

(G) Learn about acrostic poems.

English translations obscure the fact that the first four chapters of the Book of Lamentations are acrostic (uh-KROS-tik) poems (in which the first letter of each line begins with a letter of the Hebrew alphabet, in order). The fifth chapter has the same number of verses as the Hebrew alphabet has letters (22).

Scholars suggest that the acrostic style was likely used for at least two reasons: (1) to express the totality of an idea (from "a" to "z"); and (2) to assist persons in committing a poem to memory. In the Book of Lamentations, the acrostic format may also function to create some sense of control over potentially uncontrollable emotions.

- For this learning activity you will need several Bible dictionaries and commentaries on the Book of Lamentations.
- Divide class members into groups of three and four. Share with them the information given at the beginning of this learning option about acrostic style in Hebrew poetry.
- Ask groups to learn what they can about acrostic poems by looking up Lamentations in the reference books you have available.
- Ask each group to rewrite Lamentations 2:1-6 in the acrostic style. That is, begin the first line with a word

that starts with "a"; the second line with a word that starts with "b"; and so on.

- When groups have completed their research and writing, ask a representative from each group to report its findings to the class as a whole.

(H) View the Book of Lamentations from the Babylonians' point of view.

As we have seen, Israel viewed positive events (military victories, bountiful harvests, adequate rainfall) as divine blessings—indications of God's favor. By the same token, Israel regarded negative events (military defeats, famine, drought) as signs of divine displeasure.

The Babylonians also regarded positive events as divine blessings, while negative events signalled their gods' displeasure. They most certainly interpreted Jerusalem's destruction as a victory from their gods, including the mighty deity, Marduk (MAR-dyook).

- Divide class members into groups of three; provide each group with paper and pens or pencils.
- Share with them the information given at the beginning of this learning option.
- Ask each group to rewrite Lamentations 2:1-6 from the perspective of the Babylonians. Suddenly, a lament becomes a victory song!
- At the end of ten minutes, ask a spokesperson for each group to read aloud its version of Lamentations 2:1-6.

Dimension 3:
What Does the Bible Mean to Us?

(I) Look at a prophet's life.

In this learning option your class members will be reflecting on the life of a prophet. In this Volume 7 we have been primarily looking at the lives of Isaiah and Jeremiah. Since traditionally the Book of Lamentations is credited to Jeremiah, let's reflect specifically on his life.

- For this learning option you will need large sheets of paper and markers or a chalkboard and chalk.
- Ask class members to recall different events and situations in which Jeremiah found himself. As they offer these, write them on the paper or chalkboard.
- After you have listed these life events, go back and place a check mark beside the events that seemed to challenge Jeremiah's faith.
- Divide class members into pairs for sharing.
- Ask them to share with each other:

—When have you experienced rejection or mockery?

—Have you ever felt pressured to compromise your faith or Christian principles?

—Have you ever felt like you were a "prophet" crying out to people who would not listen?

—How would you feel if God told you that your town or country was going to suffer terribly because of the sins of the people?

—Today are we ever called on to be "prophets" of God? If so, when or how?

(J) Consider a shift from lament to praise.

Lamentations 3 begins with a vivid description of distress. The lamenter describes his or her plight, identified as the result of God's wrath (verses 1-20).

Suddenly, however, the poet's words shift from lament to praise. Verse 22, for example, affirms:

"The steadfast love of the LORD never ceases,
    his mercies never come to an end."

- To sample this shift recruit two readers. Ask the first reader to read Lamentations 3:1-21. Ask the second reader to read Lamentations 3:22-30.

- In the Book of Psalms, many individual and communal laments display similar shifts from profound expressions of grief and pain to assertions of trust in God. (Psalm 22 is an example of such a shift.)

- Ask class members to divide into groups of three.

- Provide each group with Bibles, pens or pencils, and paper.

- Ask each group to compose a paragraph or two reflecting their thoughts on the function of such shifts. Are both sorts of experiences—fear of divine wrath and trust in God's mercy—common to sorrowful experiences?

- One or more group members may wish to share with the group a personal experience in which he or she has experienced both types of emotions—anger at God and trust in God's mercy. Groups should encourage, but not insist upon, such sharing.

- At the end of ten minutes, ask each group to share its writings with the entire class.

(K) Compose a communal lament.

Every day's news brings word of tragic events somewhere in our world.

In our faith communities, we can raise voices of lament—expressions of sorrow, of concern for those who suffer, of frustration, and even of anger in the face of catastrophes that seem so senseless, or that vividly illustrate the consequences of human greed, oppression, and deceit.

- For this activity you will need a large sheet of paper and markers for each group to use.

- Divide class members into groups of three or four.

- Ask each group to identify a particular crisis, at home or abroad, they wish to lament in prayer to God.

- Then ask group members jointly to compose a lament concerning that crisis. Their lament need not be patterned rigidly on poems in the Book of Lamentations. Groups may reflect on God's role in the midst of suffering in ways that differ from ancient Israel's ways. And, of course, their laments may well reflect the centrality of Christ for Christian faith.

- At the end of ten minutes, invite each group to display its lament before the class as a whole.

- Taking turns, each group should lead the class in praying its lament.

(L) Close with a time of worship.

- Close your session with some quiet time for reflection on today's discussion. You may wish to read selections from Chapter 5 in the Book of Lamentations. Especially include the closing verses, 19-21.

- A psalm that conveys the messages of despair and hope is Psalm 130. Either Scripture selection would be appropriate to close this session.

Additional Bible Helps

In times of crisis, people's faith in God may be shaken to its foundations. We long for divine consolation, a sense of God's presence with us. We may also feel angry at God, wish to bargain with God, or ask God why we must walk through this "valley of the shadow of death."

In these respects, we are very much like the people of ancient Israel. When Jerusalem was destroyed and the Judean nation collapsed, the survivors faced many obstacles—physical, emotional, social, political, and military. Perhaps their greatest struggle was the struggle for faith in the midst of catastrophe. Certainly they knew that among their religious traditions were stern warnings about the consequences of sin. Other religious traditions, however, had provided the Judeans with strong bases for their conviction that God would not allow Jerusalem, when ruled the descendants of David, and the site of Yahweh's Temple, to be destroyed. Consider, for example, Psalm 48:1b-3, 8:

His holy mountain, beautiful in
    elevation,
    is the joy of all the earth,
Mount Zion, in the far north,
    the city of the great King.
Within its citadels God
    has shown himself a sure defense.
. . . .

As we have heard, so we have seen
in the city of the LORD of hosts,
in the city of our God
which God establishes forever.

When the Davidic empire came to an end and Jerusalem lay in ruins, some survivors undoubtedly concluded that faith in God had become a losing proposition, since Yahweh had obviously either been defeated by a more powerful Babylonian deity or else had simply abandoned Judah to its fate. The authors of the Book of Lamentations, however, were not among their number. Though they attributed their plight to Yahweh's just punishment for sin, they would not abandon hope of experiencing anew God's compassion and mercy.

Though our understanding of God's ways with the world is not that of ancient Israel, we have much to learn from the Book of Lamentations. Notably, we benefit from Israel's example in bringing its grief, confusion, frustra-tion, anger, and hope to God. We Christians sometimes act as if piety precluded an honest statement to God about our deepest troubles and questions. But God is with us in despair, as well as joy. God hears our prayers and loves us in the midst of tragedy, even when those prayers contain our most difficult questions about death, pain, and alienation.

Many biblical scholars believe that the Book of Job, like Lamentations, was composed in the aftermath of Jerusalem's destruction. There, in an even more prominent way, Job's laments are coupled with questions to God. Job's questions cut to the heart of Israel's most profound beliefs about God's justice and about the correlation between human righteousness and divine reward on the one hand, human sinfulness and divine punishment on the other. So the Book of Job, like Lamentations, emboldens us to address God from the depths of our despair. So too Jesus' lament from the cross: "My God, my God, why have you forsaken me?" (Mark 15:34).

ADDITIONAL RESOURCES

Five Biblical Portraits, by Elie Wiesel (University of Notre Dame Press, 1981); ISBN 0-268-00962-7.

Isaiah's Vision and the Family of God, Literary Currents in Biblical Interpretation Series; by Katheryn P. Darr (Westminster John Knox, 1994); ISBN 00-664-25537-X.

Jeremiah, The Anchor Bible Series, Volume 21; by John Bright (Doubleday & Company, 1965); ISBN 0-385-00823-6.

Lamentations: A New Translation With Introduction and Commentary. The Anchor Bible Series; by Delbert R. Hillers (Doubleday & Company, 1972); ISBN 0-385-26407-0.

The Storyteller's Companion to the Bible: Volume 7: The Prophets II, Michael E. Williams, editor (Abingdon Press, 1995); ISBN 0-687-00120-X.

Understanding the Old Testament, 4th edition; by Bernhard W. Anderson (Prentice-Hall, 1986); ISBN 0-13-935925-7.

Female City Imagery in Hebrew Poetry

By Katheryn P. Darr

Introduction

Metaphors and similes are invitations to perceive one thing through the "lens" of another. When Jeremiah says of the people of Judah, "their tongue is a deadly arrow" (9:8), we perceive the instrument of deceitful human speech as a sharp and swift weapon. Likewise, when the author of Lamentations 3 says of God, "He is a bear lying in wait for me, / a lion in hiding" (verse 10), we perceive God through the lens of vicious wild animals suddenly striking their prey with mortal wounds. In Isaiah 66:13, the simile "as a mother comforts her child" shapes our image of God comforting Jerusalem's inhabitants.

Each of the biblical books examined in this volume contains female city imagery:

- Isaiah 54:1 addresses Jerusalem as a barren woman;

- In Jeremiah 48:18, part of an oracle against Israel's enemy, Moab, the city of Dibon (DIGH-buhn) is ordered down from her throne to mourn upon parched ground;

- In Lamentations 1:2, Jerusalem sheds bitter tears in the night, with no one to comfort her.

Ancient Israel's poets were not the first to describe or address cities as females. They both adopted and adapted the poetic convention from their ancient Near Eastern neighbors. Within the Old Testament, female city imagery takes many forms and serves a variety of literary functions. Often, such tropes (figurative uses of language) are drawn from the experiences of family life. Cities appear as fair maidens, headstrong daughters, beloved wives, compassionate mothers, blatant adulteresses, and bereaved widows. These images function to convey "a sense of the love, passion, jealousy, anger, shame, and pride believed to be as integral to the relations binding God and Israel as they were to the ties binding members of human families" (*Isaiah's Vision and the Family of God*, by Katheryn Pfisterer Darr; Westminster John Knox Press, 1994; page 122).

Daughter Imagery

The phrase "daughter PN" (where PN represents the name of a city) frequently appears in biblical poetry. Why were cities represented as daughters, rather than sons? Elaine Follis offers one explanation:

"Sons commonly are thought to represent the adventuresome spirit of a society. . . . Daughters, on the other hand, have been associated with stability, with the building up of society, with nurturing the community at its very heart and center. The stereotypical male spirit lies in conquest, while the stereotypical female spirit lies in culture. . . .

"As [daughter], the city becomes the quintessence of civilization and culture, of a stable lifestyle, of permanent relationships" ("The Holy City as Daughters," in *Directions in Biblical Hebrew Poetry*; Elaine R. Follis, editor; Journal for the Study of the Old Testament Supplement Series, 40; JSOT Press, 1987; pages 176–77).

When Israel's poets addressed cities as daughters, they brought to the minds of their hearers and readers certain stereotypical ideas about female offspring. These ideas might include affection, pity, and especially vulnerability. In Isaiah 1:8, for example, the metaphor "daughter Zion" contributes to the reader's sense of Zion's isolation and vulnerability. In Lamentations 2:13, picturing Jerusalem as a daughter who has experienced physical abuse invites our sympathy. Contrast our delight for her when, in Zephaniah 3:14, daughter Zion is urged to rejoice.

Wife and Mother Imagery

In the Hebrew Scriptures, cities often appear as wives and mothers. Both Samaria (capital of Israel, the Northern Kingdom) and Jerusalem (Judah's capital) are addressed in certain contexts as Yahweh's wives and the mothers of their inhabitants. Foreign cities also are depicted as mothers, though they nowhere appear as the wives of Yahweh or of rival male deities.

The oracles of Second (Chapters 40–55) and Third (Chapters 56–66) Isaiah make frequent use of wife and mother imagery. In Isaiah 54:6-8, for example, Yahweh speaks tenderly to Jerusalem, as a husband might speak to an abandoned wife with whom he hopes to reconcile:

> For the LORD has called you
>   like a wife forsaken and grieved in spirit,
>   like the wife of a man's youth when she is cast off,
>   says your God.
> For a brief moment I abandoned you,
>   but with great compassion I will gather you.
> In overflowing wrath for a moment
>   I hid my face from you,
> but with everlasting love I will have
> compassion on you,
>   says the LORD, your Redeemer.

In Isaiah 60:4, Mother Zion is urged to lift up her eyes and witness the homecoming of her children.

In both these poems, family metaphors underscore the love, compassion, and unbreakable bonds uniting the family of God.

Adultery Imagery

In ancient Israelite society, married women were forbidden to engage in sexual intercourse with anyone except their husbands. According to Deuteronomy 22:22, adultery was a capital offense. The specter of female infidelity threatened the foundation of Israel's patriarchal society, in which inheritance normally passed from father to son. After all, if a woman became pregnant with another man's child, the land belonging to her husband's family could pass into the hands of an illegitimate heir.

In describing illicit intercourse by a wife, biblical authors not only used the verb meaning "to commit adultery" but also the verb meaning "to be a harlot." Accusing a married woman of "harlotry" intensified the infidelity charge. In Jeremiah 3:2-3, for example, the prophet accuses Jerusalem of playing the whore with many lovers (worshiping deities other than her "husband," Yahweh; seeking alliances with foreign nations).

Widowed City Imagery

References to widowed cities appear in the books of Isaiah, Jeremiah, and Lamentations. In Isaiah 47—a lengthy judgment poem that addresses Babylonia's capital city, Babylon, as a woman—the personified city boasts:

> "I am, and there is no one besides me;
> I shall not sit as a widow
>   or know the loss of children"—

But the speaker rejoins:

> both these things shall come upon you

> in a moment, in one day:
> the loss of children and widowhood
>   shall come upon you in full measure,
> in spite of your many sorceries
>   and the great power of your enchantments.
>   (Isaiah 47: 8b-9)

In Hebrew, the word translated "widow" ('almanah) bears two different meanings. In contexts concerning the marital status of a woman whose husband has died, 'almanah has the same meaning as our English word widow. But in contexts where protecting and providing for a socially disadvantaged woman is at issue, "a once married woman who has no means of financial support and who is thus in need of special legal protection" is a more precise definition ("The 'Widowed' City," by Chayim Cohen, in *The Journal of the Ancient Near Eastern Society of Columbia University*, 1973; volume 5; page 76).

In "widowed city" texts, Cohen argues, the second of these two definitions is pertinent:

> When applied to a city, this concept would undoubtedly designate a once independent city which has lost its independence and is now completely dependent upon another state for protection and survival. In short, *the "widowed" city motif seems to refer to a once independent city which has become a vassal of another state* (pages 78–79).

This meaning of 'almanah is particularly clear in Lamentations 1:1:

> How lonely sits the city
>   that once was full of people!
> How like a widow she has become,
>   she that was great among the nations!
> She that was a princess among the provinces
>   has become a vassal.

Jerusalem is not a "widow" in the conventional sense; the authors of the Hebrew Scriptures never express the possibility that Yahweh, her husband, might die. But in her present circumstances, she sits lonely and abandoned by her God, reduced to desperate straits, the least among the nations.

Conclusion

Through various types of female city imagery, biblical poets, including the prophets, invited their audiences to perceive urban centers, great and small, through the lenses of females—including their conventional roles and stereotypical ideas about them. In adopting such symbolic language, these authors sought to stir in their hearers and readers a spectrum of thoughts and emotions, from tender love to bitter rage.

The Use of Isaiah in the New Testament

By John A. Darr and Katheryn P. Darr

The earliest Christians had no "New Testament." Their holy books were the Scriptures acknowledged by all segments of Judaism in the first century A.D. Their Bible consisted wholly of what we call the Old Testament (or the Hebrew Scriptures). They were especially reliant on the Septuagint (SEP-too-uh-jint), the Greek translation of those Scriptures. We modern Christians need to reflect on the fact that those who wrote the New Testament and developed our essential religious ideas operated within the literary and theological "world" of Jewish Scriptures. To a greater degree than most of us may realize, every New Testament writing is saturated with these prior writings, whether in the form of direct quotations, references, allusions, linguistic styles, or literary models. It is virtually impossible to understand the theological arguments of early Christian authors unless one has a firm grasp of the Scriptures they presuppose. Especially important in this regard was the Book of Isaiah. Again and again, those who believed in Jesus turned to this major prophetic work as a resource to help them understand Christ. Isaiah was used to resolve ideological problems and to establish the identities of the early Christian groups in relation to other Jewish groups. In this essay we shall explore some of the ways this creative theological process worked.

Reapplying Isaiah

In one sense what the earliest Christians did with Isaiah was not new at all. We have seen in our study of the Book of Isaiah that this work itself illustrates a lengthy process of what we might call retraditioning or reshaping and reapplying them to new situations. The belief that Isaiah consistently had something authoritative and insightful to say about current affairs was firmly established in Jewish tradition long before Christians began to appropriate Isaiah to make sense of their own situation.

What made the Christians' use of Isaiah new and different was the prism of resurrection faith through which they viewed all of the ancient sacred writings. In other words, they read Isaiah as predicting and explaining the death and vindication of Jesus. Also Isaiah served to explain the development of the Christian movement out into the broader Mediterranean world of their time. In Luke's Gospel the resurrected Jesus summarizes these concerns by asserting that Moses, the prophets, and the psalmists wrote "that the Messiah is to suffer and to rise from the dead on the third day" (Luke 24:46). Also Luke's Gospel proclaims that repentance and forgiveness of sins should be preached in Jesus' name "to all nations [or, Gentiles], beginning from Jerusalem" (24:47). Behind this worldview lies the conviction from Isaiah that God controls history and has a master plan for its progression.

A "Voice Crying in the Wilderness"

The early Christians were convinced that they were living during the last days of this "salvation history." The sacred events that had transpired among them were the culmination of God's overall plan, and in Jesus, they were experiencing the outpouring of God's Spirit envisioned by Isaiah many centuries earlier. All of the Gospels begin the story of Jesus' ministry by referring to John the Baptist as the "voice crying in the wilderness" (quoted from Isaiah 40:3), the signal that, once again, God was acting decisively on behalf of God's people.

> [John] went into all the region around the Jordan, proclaiming a baptism of repentance for the forgiveness of sins, as it is written in the book of the words of the prophet Isaiah,
>> "The voice of one crying out in the
>> wilderness:

'Prepare the way of the Lord,
    make his paths straight.
Every valley shall be filled,
    and every mountain and hill shall be made
        low,
and the crooked shall be made straight,
    and the rough ways made smooth;
and all flesh shall see the salvation of
    God.' "
        (Luke 3:4-6; from Isaiah 40:3-5; also see
        Matthew 3:2-3; Mark 1:2-3; and John 1:23)

Isaiah's prediction of a miraculous return from exile for Judean captives in Babylonia here becomes a call to prepare to see Jesus, the new "salvation of God."

The Working of the Spirit
The Book of Isaiah looks toward an idyllic time when God's salvation would be plainly perceived in the working of the Spirit. At the synagogue in his hometown of Nazareth, Jesus tied this Isaianic prophecy to himself:

"The Spirit of the Lord is upon me,
    because he has anointed me
        to bring good news to the poor.
He has sent me to proclaim release to
    the captives
    and recovery of sight to the blind,
        to let the oppressed go free,
to proclaim the year of the Lord's favor."
        (Luke 4:18-19; see Isaiah 61:1-2; 58:6)

All these activities in favor of people in need were hallmarks of Jesus' ministry and of the ministry of the early church. Isaiah's words to the defeated exiles of his day spoke strongly to the early Christians. These early followers of Jesus were also persecuted and a minority both within the Roman Empire and within Judaism.

Jesus' Lack of Appeal to Jews
The latter point introduces another important usage to which Isaiah was put in the church of the first century. If, as the Christians asserted, God had begun a new and important phase of salvation history, why had so few of the chosen people seen Jesus as such? Why did only a small minority of Jews accept Jesus as Messiah? And why was the church so rapidly becoming a Gentile (non-Jewish) movement? For Christians, Isaiah's prophecy concerning God's overarching plan helped establish a sense of *continuity* with Jewish tradition, but how were they to explain the rather obvious *discontinuities* with that tradition? In their explanation of their of unique theological positions, the earliest Christians depended on Isaiah. Believers in Jesus took over Isaiah's prophecy to explain

certain circumstances in their own situations. Perhaps the most important borrowings that took place involved the arguments that (1) despite the opposition of humans, God's plan would indeed be realized, and (2) because of the condition of their "hearts" people often fail to see that God is working in new ways in their midst.

The early Christians perceived a certain irony in the fact that those who should have been the first to embrace Jesus as Messiah never did and, in fact, opposed him and his message. The chief priests, scribes, and Pharisees all had the advantage of knowing the Scriptures. Yet, according to the Gospels, they both failed to recognize Jesus and were actually antagonistic to him and his movement. How to explain that Jewish leadership groups in general opposed the plan of God in Jesus? Isaiah, who also encountered much opposition from his people's leaders, provided potent imagery for the Christians' explanation on this point. Isaiah's famous allegory of the vineyard (Isaiah 5:1-7), in which a carefully planted but unfruitful vineyard stands for Israel, was refashioned by the early church (and perhaps by Jesus himself) to place blame for the "vineyard's" failure to accept Jesus squarely on the shoulders of Jewish leaders. In Jesus' parable of the vineyard, he adds to Isaiah's imagery wicked tenant farmers (=leaders) who mismanage the farm and mistreat messengers (=prophets and Jesus) from the rightful owner (=God; Matthew 21:33-46; Mark 12:1-12; Luke 20:9-19). What gets destroyed then is not the vineyard itself (as per Isaiah), but rather the tenants (the Jewish leaders who oppose Jesus and abet his execution). In the light of the recent destruction of the Temple and its leadership by the Romans (A.D. 70), such imagery was especially potent for Christians living in the last quarter of the first century. And the notion that the "vineyard" gets turned over to "other tenants" so that God's plan is not thwarted would have struck a chord in a church witnessing a massive influx of Gentiles, but a dwindling number of Jewish followers.

Another scriptural resource for answering the question of why more Jews did not accept Jesus as the Christ was found in Isaiah 6:9-10. The tactic of using this passage for just such a purpose is illustrated brilliantly at the end of Acts. When Paul's message about Jesus is rejected by most of the Jewish leaders in Rome, he delivers this parting argument:

The Holy Spirit was right in saying to your ancestors
through the prophet Isaiah,
    "Go to this people and say,
    You will indeed listen, but never understand,
        and you will indeed look, but never
            perceive.
    For this people's heart has grown dull,
        and their ears are hard of hearing,
            and they have shut their eyes;

so that they might not look with their
　　eyes,
　and listen with their ears,
　　and understand with their heart and turn—
　　and I would heal them."
Let it be known to you then that this salvation of God
has been sent to the Gentiles; they will listen.
　　　　　　　　　(Acts 28:25b-28; from Isaiah 6:9-10)

According to early Christians (drawing heavily on Isaiah), only those with properly prepared hearts were able to recognize God's new activity in Jesus. Once again, the lack of response from Jews was considered cause enough for God's plan to encompass the Gentiles.

A Suffering Messiah
One of the most difficult tasks of early Christians was to defend the notion that the Messiah was to suffer and die a disgraceful death at the hands of the hated Roman rulers. Most Jews at the turn of the millennium thought of the Messiah as a glorious figure, a Davidic descendant who would restore the monarchy, overthrow super-power oppressors like Rome, and establish Jerusalem as the world center for the worship of God. All the nations of the earth would come to worship the true God in Jerusalem once the Messiah came. How then could the Christians claim that Jesus, a person who seemed to have no political or military ambition, who associated with tax collectors, advocated "giving to Caesar what is Caesar's," and was executed by the Romans be the long-awaited Messiah? To answer questions such as these, the early church turned to Isaiah once again. His haunting poems about the suffering servant of God (especially in Isaiah 52:13–53:12) were forever indelibly linked with Jesus' passion in the Christian imagination. The questions Isaiah asks echo eerily the skepticism the early church encountered in response to its claims about Jesus:

Who has believed what we have heard?
　And to whom has the arm of the LORD been
　　revealed?
For . . . he had no form or majesty
　　that we should look at him,
　nothing in his appearance that we should
　　desire him.
He was despised and rejected by others;
　a man of suffering and acquainted with
　　infirmity;
and as one from whom others hide their faces
　he was despised, and we held him of no
　　account.
　　　　　　　　　(Isaiah 53:1-3)

The suffering servant passages became a treasure trove of material for justifying both the fact and the manner of

Jesus' death. Why was he condemned? It was a miscarriage of justice: "By a perversion of justice was he taken away" (Isaiah 53:8). Why did he not defend himself against the charges? His silence was predicted by Isaiah: "He was oppressed, and he was afflicted, / yet he did not open his mouth" (53:7a). If he was innocent, why was he executed with criminals? "[He] was numbered with the transgressors" (53:12); "They made his grave with the wicked . . . / although he had done no violence, / and there was no deceit in his mouth" (53:9). Why then would God allow such a thing to happen to a righteous person? What function might such suffering have?

Surely he has borne our infirmities
　and carried our diseases;
yet we accounted him stricken,
　struck down by God, and afflicted.
But he was wounded for our transgressions,
　crushed for our iniquities;
upon him was the punishment that made us
　　whole,
and by his bruises we are healed.
All we like sheep have gone astray;
　we have all turned to our own way,
and the LORD has laid on him the iniquity
　of us all.
　　　　　　　　　(Isaiah 53:4-6)

The New Testament notion of Christ's suffering being done on our sinful behalf is thus grounded in the servant songs of Second Isaiah. The theological doctrine of Christ and the Christian understanding of salvation owe a great debt to the ancient prophetic writing of Isaiah.

Conclusion
In conclusion, our short sketch of ways in which Isaiah was used by the writers of the New Testament evokes— but certainly does not exhaust—the richness of that creative weaving of our biblical texts. Isaiah was particularly helpful for the early Christians as they sought to establish their identity over against other groups and to defend their fundamental beliefs in a hostile environment. Perhaps better than any other book in the Hebrew Scriptures, Isaiah served to legitimate Christian claims concerning Jesus and to confirm their movement's place in the plan of God.

ADDITIONAL RESOURCES
See page 67 for additional resources to use with this study.

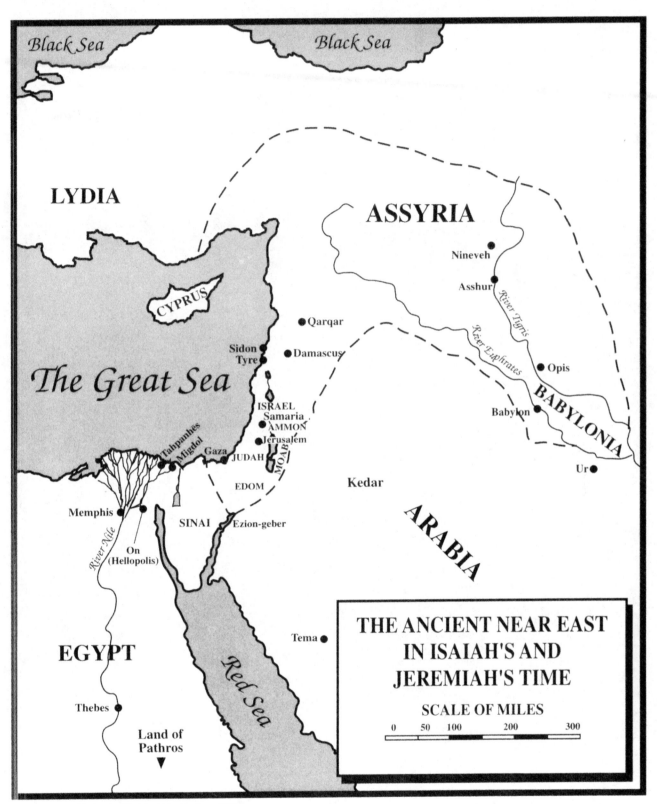

THE ANCIENT NEAR EAST
IN ISAIAH'S AND
JEREMIAH'S TIME

SCALE OF MILES

0   50   100   200   300

CPSIA information can be obtained
at www.ICGtesting.com
Printed in the USA
FSOW03n1935130217
30786FS